Prayer for Relief: ChatGPT

"When truth is silenced by power, and justice drowns in paperwork, the only way forward is to speak louder—with evidence, with clarity, and now—with code."

— Prayer for Relief: ChatGPT

First Edition
Printed in the United States of America

For more information or permissions, contact:
Wilhelm Haberkorn
Email: DonauLLC@protonmail.com

Disclaimer

This book is a work of nonfiction. It is based on real events, legal proceedings, and personal experiences. The primary facts, court filings, and legal arguments have been drawn from publicly available records and firsthand documentation.

However, to ensure privacy, protect individuals not central to the legal narrative, and preempt potential legal disputes or retaliatory claims, **some names, timelines, and identifying details have been modified or condensed**. Certain facts may have been reordered or slightly altered for clarity, emphasis, or narrative cohesion.

Any such alterations do not affect the essential truth of the story, the legal issues raised, or the educational purpose of this work.

This book is intended for informational and educational purposes only. It is not legal advice. While it offers guidance for pro se litigants and those navigating private institutional governance, readers are strongly encouraged to consult a licensed attorney regarding their specific legal concerns.

The use of AI technologies, including ChatGPT, as described in this book, is intended to demonstrate accessible legal support tools for individuals acting in good faith. Results may vary based on context, jurisdiction, and platform capability.

Any resemblance to actual people or events not directly named or referenced is purely coincidental or altered for privacy and legal precaution.

Foreword

For Every Silenced Member Whose Name Was Never Even Mentioned

In every generation, some stories pierce public silence—not because they are the loudest, but because they speak a truth that institutions have long buried beneath ritual, protocol, and paper. *Prayer for Relief: ChatGPT* is one such story.

This book is not a memoir.
It is not a legal manual.
It is not a rant.

It is, quite simply, a roadmap for anyone who has been erased by power and told to accept it.
Especially those who were never even mentioned in the letter.

At the center of this story are Wilhelm and Susanne Haberkorn: two active, engaged members of The Club on Skidaway Island, Georgia. For 24 years, they built their retirement with intention—enjoying golf, tennis, community, nature, and friendship. Susanne was not just Wilhelm's wife. She was a force in her own right: a celebrated tennis player, a social bridge builder, and a vital part of the very fabric that The Club claimed to cherish.

Then came the fall.

On September 11, 2021, Susanne suffered a serious hip injury on a poorly maintained court. The Club responded with silence. No investigation. No incident report. No apology. Just bureaucratic evasion. And when Wilhelm, seeking accountability, posted a calm and factual message in the member forum, he was expelled within 48 hours—**without warning, without hearing, without evidence.**

And then, without so much as a mention, Susanne was expelled too.

She had done nothing. Said nothing. Filed no claim.
She was simply **removed by association**.

No letter. No due process. No acknowledgment.

Why? Because The Club—and clubs like it—**treat spouses not as members, but as dependents**.

And this, perhaps more than any other part of this story, is why this book had to be written.

To every woman whose name never made it into the minutes:
To every spouse whose access was revoked silently:
To every member treated like an accessory rather than an equal—this book is **for you**.

Susanne was not a dependent.
She was a co-member, as stated in The Club's own membership certificate. See Appendix C.

Like so many women in private clubs across the country, she paid dues, organized events, maintained friendships, and built the very community that would later erase her.

This book is your warning—and your tool.

Because if it happened to Susanne, it can happen to you.

You may think your good standing protects you.
You may think your decades of contribution count.
You may think your name on the account guarantees fairness.

But in systems where procedure trumps principle, **a quiet spouse is the easiest member to erase**.

And for those thinking, *"Surely the courts would intervene?"*
Think again.

This book also tells the story of how **intra-corporate privilege**—a legal doctrine designed to protect internal corporate deliberations—was weaponized not to protect justice, but to prevent it.

When Wilhelm filed a defamation claim against The Club for labeling his measured, factual forum post a "legal threat," The Club never defended what it said.
They didn't have to.

They simply invoked **intra-corporate privilege**, and the court agreed.

What does that mean?

It means that even though The Club's defamatory statements about Wilhelm were distributed beyond leadership and caused reputational harm…

Even though the accusation of making a "legal threat" was **completely unsupported** by the text of the forum post…

Even though The Club confiscated nearly **$30,000** in member equity from Wilhelm like a common thief…

The court refused to hear any of it.

Because the statements were made "within the corporation," and therefore shielded from scrutiny.

No finding of truth.
No examination of motive.
No ruling on substance.

Just a gavel and a wall.

That's what intra-corporate privilege means today:
A Club can say anything, do anything, and damage anyone—so long as it claims the statements were "internal."

This isn't legal nuance.

This is a red flag for every existing and prospective Club member across the country.

If you're considering joining a private Club—The Club or any other—check the court records.

See if that Club has:

- Expelled members without hearings.
- Invoked privilege to avoid defamation liability.
- Withheld or deleted records.
- Silenced spouses without so much as a name mentioned.

- Taken thousands of dollars and called it policy.

Because if they have, you're not walking into a community.

You're walking into a trap.

This book exists to make those traps **visible**.

The Haberkorns weren't asking for special treatment.

They were asking to be heard.

They were asking to understand why decades of loyal membership could be erased in two days.

They were asking why the people who had once welcomed them with handshakes were now watching in silence.

They were asking, *"Is this justice?"*

And when The Club said nothing,
When the courts said, "You filed too late,"
When the law prioritized power over truth…

They turned to something the system didn't expect.

Artificial intelligence.

ChatGPT didn't solve everything.

But it changed everything.

It gave Wilhelm the ability to:

- Understand the law.
- Draft motions.
- Prepare responses.
- Build timelines.
- Anticipate defenses.
- Ask more intelligent questions.
- Sound like someone the court had to listen to—even if it didn't want to.

It didn't just help him speak.
It helped him **speak in their language**.

And in doing so, it made his truth **impossible to ignore**.

This book is a direct result of that transformation.

It is built from filings.
From prompts.
From nights spent dissecting statutes, formatting briefs, organizing exhibits.

It is not theory.
It is not wishful thinking.
It is **battle-tested clarity**.

And now, it's yours.

To the silent spouse.
To the erased co-member.
To the persistent litigant.
To the hopeful whistleblower.
To the person with no lawyer, no budget, and no time—

This book is your blueprint.

It will show you:

- How to prompt ChatGPT as your co-counsel.
- How to fight back without losing your mind—or your money.
- How to protect your rights with precision.
- How to preserve your record, even if the court tries to ignore it.

Because justice doesn't always come from the bench.
Sometimes, it comes from **you**.

Prayer for Relief is more than a legal phrase.

It is the last line in your complaint.

It is what you ask for when they've taken what they weren't supposed to touch.

It is what you file when they think you'll just go away.

It is what Susanne never got.
And what Wilhelm had to fight for, **with code as his sword**.

And now?

It's what you carry in your hands.

A book.
A toolkit.

A prompt engine.
A story that cannot be erased.

Let this be the last time anyone calls you dependent.

Let this be the last time they take your voice.

Let this be the start of something louder.

Welcome to Prayer for Relief.

— Wilhelm Haberkorn
(84-year-old self-represented litigant)
(Who says that you are too old to learn)

"They used privilege to silence truth. This book gives truth its voice back."

— Prayer for Relief: ChatGPT

The Island of Compassion

A Tribute to the Women Who Remembered What The Club Forgot

In the long, painful story that unfolds in these pages, no one suffered more than **Susanne Haberkorn**.

An accidental fall on Club property. A fractured hip. The silent onset of dementia. A sudden, faceless expulsion. And then, the collapse of a 24-year world she helped build.

But perhaps what hurt most wasn't the injury or the letter.

It was the silence.

From neighbors. From clubmates. From a community that once cheered her championship volleys and shared her tennis courts.

They looked away.

They told themselves it wasn't their fight.

They chose comfort over character.

But not everyone did.

In a world that had turned cold, **a few women refused to let compassion die**.

They stood quietly. But they stood **firmly**.

They took action—not for glory, not for credit—but out of love, loyalty, and something that seems rarer every day: **decency**.

- **Kathleen** and **Tanis** defied the expulsion order in the most elegant of ways—by taking Susanne to lunch on Club property. Not in protest, but in honor. In memory of who she was, who she is, and what friendship once meant inside those gates.
- **Christine** and **Inge** likewise offered continued presence—not in headlines, but in hugs, in time, in unwavering inclusion.
- From afar, **Traudl** in Clemson, South Carolina, calls Susanne regularly. She asks nothing. She gives everything: connection.
- And **Gayle** in Oconomowoc, Wisconsin, reaches across five decades of friendship to maintain a bond that time, distance, and even institutional cruelty could not sever.

These are **women of character**.

They remind us that humanity does not require a bylaw.

Compassion does not wait for permission.

Their names deserve to live in these pages, not for accolades, but because they chose **integrity over fear**, **kindness over conformity**, and **connection over silence**.

In a club that abandoned its own values, they **honored them**.

And in doing so, they gave Susanne something no ruling could revoke: **Dignity.**

"They didn't protest. They didn't grandstand. They remembered Susanne—and in doing so, they remembered what The Club forgot: its soul."

— Prayer for Relief: ChatGPT

🗺 Reader Map

Welcome to *Prayer for Relief: ChatGPT*—a book that serves many kinds of readers, from private club members to legal professionals, from the curious to the courageous pro se litigant, and from the AI beginner to the prompt engineer in training. While this book tells one compelling story of injustice at The Club, it is also a gateway into a much larger world of using AI to understand, navigate, and even challenge legal systems.

Because the audience for this book is as diverse as the problems it addresses, this **Reader Map** offers suggested pathways through the chapters. Feel free to skip around. You don't have to read every page to find value. But when you're ready, the whole book is here for you.

🏌 For The Club Members or Prospective Members:

If you're concerned about the governance, rules enforcement, or fairness within The Club—or if you're considering joining—you'll want to start with the story itself. This is where the journey began.

📌 **Start Here:**

- **Part I: Illusion**
- **Part II: Reality**
- **Part III: Legality**

📌 **Optional Extras:**

- **Appendix A: FORUM Post**

- **Appendix B: Expulsion Letter**
- **Appendix C: Membership Agreement**

🎩 For Members or Prospective Members of Other Private Clubs:

If you're part of—or thinking about joining—a private club elsewhere, you'll find cautionary lessons and empowering tools here. The story of The Club is a case study in what can go wrong—and how to protect yourself.

📌 **Start Here:**

- **Part I: Illusion**
- **Part II: Reality**
- **Part III: Legality**

📌 **Optional Extras:**

- **Appendix A: FORUM Post**
- **Appendix B: Expulsion Letter**
- **Appendix C: Membership Agreement**

⚖️ For Pro Se Litigants Focused on Private Clubs:

You are not alone. This book offers hope and help. If you're fighting your own legal battles without a lawyer, especially in the context of a club or HOA, these chapters will show you what's possible—and how AI can amplify your efforts.

📌 **Start Here:**

- **Part III: Legality**
- **Part IV: Relief**
- **Part V: Prophecy**

📌 **Optional Extras:**

- **Appendix D: All 16 Court Cases**
- **Appendix E: All Cases - Paper Volume**

⚖️ For Pro Se Litigants Dealing with General Civil Matters:

Your fight may not involve a club—but the legal principles and AI tools discussed here will still help. Skip The Club drama and jump into the chapters that equip you to draft, research, and argue more effectively.

📌 **Start Here:**

- **Part III: Legality**
- **Part IV: Relief**
- **Part II: Prophecy**

📌 **Optional Extras:**

- **Appendix D: All 16 Court Cases**
- **Appendix E: All Cases - Paper Volume**

🧠 For Curious Citizens Who Love Unusual Legal Stories:

You're here for the narrative—and you'll get a wild, true legal tale filled with twists, injustice, and courage. Enjoy the drama. Learn about how seemingly small events can unravel into big fights for fairness.

📌 **Start Here:**

- **Part I: Illusion**
- **Part II: Reality**
- **Part III: Legality**
- **Part IV: Relief**

👩‍⚖️ For Legal Professionals Exploring AI in the Law:

If you're a lawyer, paralegal, or law student curious (or skeptical) about how generative AI fits into your world, the back half of the book is your playground. You'll find both practical insights and future-focused analysis.

📌 **Start Here:**

- **Part III: Legality**
- **Part IV: Relief**
- **Part V: Prophecy**

📌 **Don't Miss:**

- **Appendix D: All 16 Court Cases**
- **Appendix E: All Cases Paper Volume**

For Beginners Learning to Use ChatGPT for Legal Work:

If you're trying to understand *how* to actually use ChatGPT to help yourself, this is your action manual. You'll learn about building prompts, feeding in facts, generating filings, and even strategizing your case.

Start Here:

- **Part III: Legality**
- **Part IV: Relief**

Toolkit:

- **Appendix D: All 16 Court Cases**
- **Appendix E: All Cases Paper Volume**

For Futurists and Reform-Minded Readers:

This book concludes with a look forward: to a future in which AI might democratize access to justice, reshape legal education, and even transform our understanding of law. If you're interested in the tectonic shifts to come, go here:

Start Here:

- **Part III: Legality**
- **Part IV: Relief**
- **Part II: Prophecy**

Want to Read Cover to Cover?

You're in for a powerful, well-rounded experience. Begin with **the Disclaimer**, and read through to the **Final Chapter: Prayer Answered**. You'll learn the story, master the tools, and see the future.

Final Tip: Every chapter includes actionable takeaways. You can use the table of contents (TOC) and appendices to revisit specific topics or refer to templates later. The goal is not just to read—but to *do*. But most importantly, start thinking about how to apply the AI capabilities to other valuable applications or problems you encounter. The sky is the limit.

Let this book be your ally.

> *"This isn't just the story of a Club—it's a gateway to understanding the system, speaking its language, and rewriting its rules."*
>
> — Prayer for Relief: ChatGPT

Part I: Illusion

The 24-Year Blissful Retirement at The Club

Chapter 1: The Dream

A Paradise That Promised Peace and Delivered Betrayal

For twenty-four years, Wilhelm and Susanne Haberkorn lived the American dream of retirement. Their home on Skidaway Island, nestled within the gates of The Club community in Savannah, Georgia, represented more than real estate—it embodied a lifetime of hard work rewarded with peace, play, and purpose. Every sunrise over the marshes felt like a blessing. Every tennis match, golf round, or dinner at The Club reinforced a belief that they had found something rare and enduring.

They were not just residents—they were *members* in the truest sense of the word. Not only did they belong, they contributed. Wilhelm brought the intellectual rigor of a well-traveled businessman to his social circles. Susanne—athletic, graceful, beloved—had become a fixture of The Club's tennis community, her racquet as reliable as her laughter. Together, they wove themselves into the fabric of The Club. Their retirement wasn't just serene—it was **purposeful, joyful, and deeply connected**.

The Promise of Belonging

Skidaway Island offered more than amenities. It offered belonging. Residents didn't just live near one another—they *lived with* one another. Golf foursomes turned into dinner parties. Tennis partners became lifelong friends. The Club served as both social catalyst and sanctuary. Where others might age in isolation, the Haberkorns thrived in fellowship.

Wilhelm found intellectual stimulation and robust conversation. Susanne found a rhythm in routine—her calendar dotted with tennis matches, fitness classes, and themed Club nights. They celebrated birthdays, anniversaries, and holidays surrounded by people who felt like family.

They had arrived at what many retirees only hope to find: **a final chapter that felt like a reward**.

But paradise has its illusions.

And as the coming chapters will show, the very institution that once nurtured their golden years would later betray their trust, expel them without process, and erase their membership with the cold precision of bureaucracy—triggering a legal war they never asked for, but refused to lose quietly.

The Fragility of Institutional Trust

In retrospect, the warning signs were always there—hidden beneath the glossy brochures and the neighborly smiles. The Club, like so many private institutions, operated under rules it could interpret or ignore at will. Governance wasn't transparent. Accountability was selective. And when tested, The Club revealed its true nature—not as a community of equals, but as a corporate entity whose first instinct was **self-preservation**, not justice.

But during those twenty-four years, none of that was visible. Not to Wilhelm. Not to Susanne. And certainly not to the many others who still live under the illusion that their membership is a shield, not a sword pointed inward.

It's easy to believe in the dream when the weather is perfect, the courts are pristine, and your neighbors are laughing. That's the seduction of places like The Club. They sell *security*. They sell *status*. They sell a future without conflict.

But they cannot deliver what they do not protect.

A Quiet Before the Legal Storm

Before the forum post. Before the fall. Before the betrayal, there were sunrise bike rides. Happy hours by the lagoon. Days that began with yoga and ended with dancing. Wilhelm and Susanne had found a rhythm of life that many envy but few achieve.

They earned it. They paid for it. They believed in it.

And yet, all it took was **one accident, one forum post, one Executive Director's decision**, and the dream shattered. The couple who had embodied the spirit of The Club for nearly a quarter of a century were cast out, silenced, and dismissed.

The story of how that happened begins not with conflict, but with peace. Not with legal filings, but with trust.

And that's why this chapter matters. Because to understand the injustice that followed, the reader must first feel the weight of what was lost—not just a membership, but a way of life.

In the next chapter, **"Golfing Glory,"** we'll follow Wilhelm onto the courses where friendships were forged and reputations built. Golf wasn't just a hobby. It was a language, a ritual, and a rite of passage within The Club—a source of identity and belonging that made what came later all the more devastating.

Before they became litigants, the Haberkorns were like anyone who believes in the promise of community.

And that illusion made the betrayal even more profound.

> *"They thought they had arrived in paradise. They didn't yet know how fragile paradise could be."*

— Prayer for Relief: ChatGPT

Chapter 2: Golfing Glory

When Friendship Fails the Fairway

Golf was never just about the scorecard. For Wilhelm Haberkorn, it was the language of trust, the rhythm of retirement, and the living proof that life after the hustle could still be filled with dignity, camaraderie, and purpose. At The Club, nestled amid the moss-draped oaks and glistening lagoons of Skidaway Island, he found what so many spend their lives chasing: community.

He didn't just join a club. He became a part of a living, breathing society. A society bound not just by bylaws and membership tiers, but by the unspoken codes of sportsmanship, mutual respect, and shared rituals.

The golf course was the sanctuary.

Each round was a ceremony. A greeting at the tee box, shared jokes in the cart, solemn nods at long putts, and the clink of glasses back at The Clubhouse bar. It was a sacred space where everyone was equal in address, regardless of how large their home or how long their résumé was. Your real handicap wasn't what you posted on the board—it was how you treated the people walking beside you.

And for over two decades, Wilhelm walked those fairways with joy, pride, and a deep sense of belonging.

A Brotherhood in Motion

His golf partners were not acquaintances. They were his circle—men who had spent careers leading businesses, navigating complexity, and commanding respect. Yet on the green, their titles were set aside. Out there, everyone played the same game by the same rules. A missed putt earned a groan, not judgment. A perfectly placed drive garnered genuine applause. These men celebrated birthdays, toasted anniversaries, and checked in after surgeries. They swapped stories, coached one another through swing slumps and aging knees, and competed fiercely, but fairly.

Golf, for them, wasn't a distraction from life—it *was* life.

And within that circle, Wilhelm was known as a player who cared not only about his game, but about the integrity of the group. He played honestly. He complimented generously. He knew the rules, followed them, and encouraged others to do the same.

It's what made his sudden expulsion from The Club all the more incomprehensible—and the silence of his golfing comrades all the more devastating.

The Swing of Loyalty

When The Club expelled Wilhelm in July 2022—just two days after he posted a short, factual forum message seeking transparency about his wife Susanne's accident—he expected, at the very least, a moment of pause from his fellow members.

He didn't ask them to protest.

He didn't expect them to resign in solidarity.

But he *did* expect someone—*anyone*—to raise a hand and say, "This doesn't make sense."

He waited for a text. For an email. For a quiet knock at his door.

None came.

The Deafening Quiet

The silence didn't arrive all at once. It arrived in stages. A missed golf invite here. A quiet distancing there. Then came the true erasure: his name removed from The Club's event roster. His tee times were canceled. His profile deleted from The Club's portal. As if 24 years of friendship, loyalty, and contribution had evaporated overnight.

The very people who had toasted with him, traded jokes with him on the 9th hole, and celebrated holiday dinners with him—said nothing. Did nothing.

And that silence spoke louder than any disciplinary letter or board decision ever could.

Because silence, in moments of injustice, is not neutral.

It is complicity.

It is an endorsement.

It is the polite, country-club version of banishment.

When Principles Go Quiet

What was perhaps most haunting wasn't The Club's corporate coldness. It was the retreat of the people who had known Wilhelm as more than a golfer—as a man of principle. These were not strangers. These were men who had seen him console a grieving friend after a spouse's passing. Who had seen him volunteer for events, help organize fundraisers, and advocate for safety improvements after Susanne's injury.

They had been witnesses not only to his swing, but to his character.

And yet, when The Club accused him—wrongly—of threatening legal action in his 22-minute forum post, not one of them requested that the post be shared or reviewed. When The Club expelled him without notice or hearing, not one of them requested an explanation.

They didn't just fail to stand up.

They refused to even *look.*

And in doing so, they upheld a system where silence protects power and loyalty ends when things get uncomfortable.

The Hidden Rules of Privilege

This wasn't just cowardice. It was a symptom of the unspoken pact that governs many elite communities: protect the institution at all costs. The rules are not always written in the bylaws. They are whispered in hallways, passed along at luncheons, and conveyed through subtle gestures.

The rules say: Don't stir trouble.

Don't question leadership.

Don't align yourself with someone who's being "difficult."

And most of all, don't challenge the illusion of perfection that allows The Club to keep its real estate brochures glossy and its membership list clean.

Wilhelm didn't violate Club rules.

He violated the illusion.

He broke the silence that others worked so hard to maintain.

When Community Becomes a Stage

Retirement communities like The Club sell a dream—one of leisure, luxury, and lifelong friendships. But what they rarely admit is that this dream often requires conformity. It thrives on selective memory and willful blindness.

To stay in The Club's good graces, one must perform.

Smile at the bar. Compliment the board. Ignore the injustice.

It's not that the other members didn't care. Some did. Quietly. Privately. A few muttered discomfort. A couple offered vague apologies when they saw Wilhelm at the grocery store. But no one dared to write a letter. No one showed up to challenge the board. No one asked questions that might jeopardize their own standing.

Because in a place like The Club, harmony is more important than justice.

And harmony, tragically, is often built on the backs of those who are sacrificed to preserve it.

Golf as a Mirror

Golf teaches patience, humility, and self-reflection. It asks its players to call penalties on themselves, to accept bad bounces with grace, and to walk the course with dignity whether they win or lose.

Wilhelm embraced those values.

But in the moment he needed the game's moral code most—in the boardroom, in The Club's governance process—it vanished.

The Club abandoned the very principles its members practiced every Saturday morning.

It wasn't just Wilhelm who was expelled.

It was everything the game was meant to represent.

A Game Played Without Honor

After the expulsion, Wilhelm's clubs remained in the garage, untouched.

It wasn't about the game anymore.

It was about what the game had hidden—the quiet compliance, the performative friendships, the institution's preference for comfort over truth.

The fairways no longer whispered peace. They echoed betrayal.

The silence of his friends, once soothing and reflective between shots, now felt loaded with avoidance. With cowardice. With a collective shrug that said, "It's not our fight."

But what none of them realized was that by failing to speak, they surrendered their integrity just as surely as Wilhelm had defended his.

He had been expelled.

They had just *exited*—morally, ethically, and spiritually—from the values they once shared.

In the next chapter, **"Tennis Legacy,"** we turn from fairways to hard courts. There, we'll meet Susanne—not just as a wife or a footnote to an accident, but as a vibrant athlete, a leader, and a beloved presence whose own erasure came not through process, but by **default**.

Her expulsion didn't come with justification. It came with **neglect**, a consequence not of who she was, but of who dared to speak beside her.

Because in this Club, silence isn't just complicity.
It's policy.

"They found community on the course, but silence in The Clubhouse when it mattered most."

— Prayer for Relief: ChatGPT

Chapter 3: Tennis Legacy

When Grace, Grit, and a Racquet Built a Community

If Wilhelm found his place on the fairways of The Club, **Susanne made the tennis courts her kingdom**. Not through ego or dominance—but through excellence, grace, and a magnetic warmth that drew others to her like a beacon.

To call Susanne a "tennis player" would be to miss the point. She wasn't simply another retiree chasing points on a sunlit court. She was **a leader, a mentor, a quiet architect of community** whose legacy stretched far beyond her strokes and footwork.

She was known not just for her agility, her deadly cross-court backhand, or her four straight Husband-and-Wife Championship wins with Wilhelm, but for her consistency in something even rarer: kindness under pressure.

On Skidaway Island, where reputations sometimes echoed louder than rallies, **Susanne's name was synonymous with sportsmanship, humility, and joy**.

The Rhythm of a Life on Court

Tennis shaped the cadence of her days. From early morning drills to doubles matches with familiar faces, to late-afternoon mixers that melted into sunset social hours, Susanne thrived in the pattern of court life. She helped organize tournaments, mentored new players, and supported those struggling with injuries or confidence.

She wasn't the loudest. She wasn't the flashiest. But she was *everywhere*—the reliable partner, the encouraging presence, the friendly face who turned what could be a competitive, sometimes cliquish, space into a sanctuary of camaraderie.

Everyone knew her. Everyone respected her.

She remembered birthdays. She sent cards to those recovering from surgery. She offered rides to out-of-town matches. She **showed up**, and in doing so, she anchored a tennis community that could have easily drifted into exclusion or pretension.

And when she wasn't on the court? She was cheering from the sidelines—always with a visor, always with a smile.

Four-Time Champion. Full-Time Partner.

Susanne's legacy found its most public stage during the annual **Husband-and-Wife Championship**—a no-handicap, alternating-shot gauntlet that tested not just skill, but *partnership*. Most couples cracked under the pressure. Many came in smiling and left with bruised egos.

Not Susanne and Wilhelm.

Together, they won the tournament four times. Not just because they were skilled (though they were), but because they knew how to move as one. There were no barked instructions. No eye rolls after missed shots. No blame.

Instead, there were shared smiles, gentle nudges, and the kind of mutual trust that made even a tough match feel joyful.

They embodied what most couples aspired to, both on and off the court.

Their dynamic became lore within The Club—**a model not just of athletic synergy, but of emotional intelligence, support, and unshakeable mutual respect**.

They weren't just winners. They were an inspiration.

The Heart of a Community

New members often found their way to Susanne. She had a way of making people feel like they belonged—like they weren't outsiders, no matter how new they were to the game or the community. She'd introduce them to others, offer to rally, suggest which clinics to join, or connect them with a group at their level.

For women especially, Susanne was more than a tennis partner—she was a *bridge*. A connector. Someone who made sure that no one sat alone on the bench or walked off the court unnoticed.

Her friendship was quiet yet profound. Her influence, though rarely acknowledged, was vast and genuine.

She didn't play for applause. She played for connection.

And in that, **she became irreplaceable**.

The Injury That Changed Everything

On September 11, 2021, that rhythm broke.

What should have been a routine doubles match ended in catastrophe. The line tape on Court #19 had come loose—a hazard she'd navigated many times before, but this time, it caught her off guard. Susanne fell hard, breaking her hip in a way that would alter not just her mobility, but the arc of her life.

In that moment, everything changed.

The Club, the courts, and the community that had once embraced her offered **no apology, no inquiry, no support**. Not even a call from management.

An accident, caused by negligence, was met with silence. And Susanne—the woman who had lifted so many others—was left to recover in isolation, without acknowledgment, and ultimately without the home she had helped build.

Collateral Damage with a Lifetime of Loyalty

What followed was a chilling testament to how institutions discard even their best.

When Wilhelm dared to post a simple message seeking transparency, it was deleted within 22 minutes. Two days later, he was expelled.

And Susanne?

She was never even named.

No letter. No hearing. No bylaw cited. She was erased—not for something she did, but because she shared a life with someone The Club had deemed inconvenient.

For all her service, all her love, all her leadership—
Susanne was expelled by default.

She was collateral damage in a campaign to silence dissent, written out of membership like she had never mattered.

And no one stood up.

No one on the tennis committee asked why.

No one demanded due process for her.

No one from the community she helped shape lifted their voice.

Her name, once spoken with admiration, became unspoken—because speaking it would mean **admitting The Club had done something unforgivable**.

When Legacy Isn't Enough

Susanne had once filled courts with laughter, movement, and grace.

Now, her absence was explained away.

People whispered, avoided, and rationalized.

Some said, "It's complicated."

Some said, "Let it go."

Some said nothing at all.

But those who once called her Superwoman knew the truth: *She had been wronged.*

Her injury. Her erasure. Her exile.

None of it was earned. None of it was defensible. And none of it was ever addressed.

The Club moved on.

But the courts never felt the same.

A Silent Court, A Deafening Message

Susanne now walks those same paths with the aid of a cane.

Her hip has healed, but her relationship with The Club—the place where she gave so much—is permanently broken.

She doesn't ask for her titles back.

She doesn't want a ceremony.

What she wants—what she *deserves*—is acknowledgment.

But it will never come. Because to acknowledge her would be to admit fault. To concede that The Club turned against its own.

So the courts remain silent. The benches empty. The community still plays, but the joy that once defined those games has dulled.

Her story, once one of triumph, became one of loss—not just of mobility, but of belonging.

She was once their Superwoman.

And they let her fall—*twice*.

In the next chapter, **“Social Circles,”** we’ll explore how The Club’s social ecosystem, once built on shared experiences and collective joy, reacted when the Haberkorns were cast out.

What happened to the dinner invitations? The celebrations? The traditions?

When justice is denied, the first thing to disappear is friendship.

“Her legacy was strength. Her punishment was silence.”

— Prayer for Relief: ChatGPT

Chapter 4: Social Circles

When the Music Stopped and the Chairs Were Gone

There is a particular kind of grief that comes not from death or violence, but from quiet abandonment. It is a grief born not from what was taken in a single blow, but from what is allowed to vanish without explanation or defense slowly.

This was the grief that settled over Wilhelm and Susanne Haberkorn after they were expelled from The Club. It wasn't just a membership that ended—it was a life. A rhythm. A calendar filled with birthdays, anniversaries, holiday parties, and golf dinners that abruptly disappeared, not because the dates changed, but because **they were no longer invited**.

This was the unraveling of **social belonging**, the silent dismantling of decades of community.

A Community of Rituals

For 24 years, the Haberkorns were at the heart of Skidaway Island's social life. From wine tastings to gala nights, from tennis mixers to charity auctions, they had built more than friendships—they had built *traditions*.

There were the annual holiday dinners with the same couples, always seated at the corner table under the chandelier in the ballroom. There were the Fourth of July cookouts with sparklers passed between grandkids, stories retold, and photographs that grew in frames year after year. There were weekly dinners at The Club, where familiar voices filled the room and the maître d' knew their preferences before they spoke.

These events weren't just social occasions. They were **affirmations of inclusion**—reminders that they were not just residents, but *insiders*. The Club was their social cathedral, and these gatherings were its Sunday services.

Then, with a single forum post and an expulsion letter, the pews emptied.

The Invitations That Stopped

At first, it was subtle.

An email thread about an upcoming dinner—one they had always attended—no longer included Wilhelm's name.

A group lunch following a doubles match went on without Susanne, though she had attended for years.

A text chain full of warm emoji reactions and shared memories went silent.

Then came the unmistakable signs. A party thrown by a couple they had once vacationed with—no invitation. A birthday bash for a close friend—held in The Clubhouse, the place they were now banned from. Friends who had once called weekly now "got busy." A neighbor who had always waved suddenly turned away.

The exile wasn't formal.

It was **social surgery**, precise and painless—for everyone except the ones removed.

The Fear of Association

What shocked Wilhelm most wasn't the betrayal of management or the Board.

It was the speed with which **their friends fell in line**.

Longtime neighbors—people who had clinked glasses with them, danced beside them, and toasted their successes—disappeared without confrontation or clarity. They didn't ask questions. They didn't offer explanations. They just **withdrew**, as if knowing them had become too heavy a burden.

Why?

Because in a place like The Club, **association is currency**.

And when someone is deemed a problem—whether justified or not—that association becomes toxic. To question The Club's decision is to risk being painted with the same brush. And so, self-preservation wins.

Old friends become neutral.

Neutral becomes distance.

Distance becomes silence.

And silence becomes **complicity**.

The Social Death Sentence

This wasn't just about exclusion from parties or events. It was a deeper, more primal kind of isolation: **being erased from the shared memory of a place you helped shape**.

Wilhelm and Susanne had hosted countless dinners, opened their home, organized fundraisers, and even offered help to members during difficult times. But in the blink of an administrative meeting, all of that was forgotten.

They had become pariahs—not because of who they were, but because of what The Club had **decided** they represented: *disruption. Conflict. Legal liability*.

And so, the couple once regarded as integral members of the social fabric was **cut out of the pattern**.

Even their grandchild, once welcomed into The Club with warmth, was no longer seen at holiday brunches or poolside barbecues. Susanne, who had delighted in showing off her tennis skills to the younger generation, now watched from outside the gates as others enjoyed the life she helped cultivate.

She had not just lost access. She had lost **acknowledgment**.

The Weaponization of Politeness

One of the cruelest realities of this social collapse was that it did not arrive with anger or accusation. It arrived with **politeness**.

With avoidance disguised as respect.

With "We miss you!" texts that never followed up.

With "So sorry to hear" comments that led nowhere.

With smiles at the grocery store that vanished once the aisle was cleared.

The Club didn't need to tell anyone to shun them. It had only to signal that they were no longer welcome.

The rest happened naturally, through the mechanism of **institutional etiquette**.

Because the greatest sin in many elite communities is not injustice—it is *disruption*. And Wilhelm and Susanne had, simply by asking for accountability, disrupted The Club's illusion of perfection.

Who They Were vs. Who They Became

It would be easier if Wilhelm and Susanne had actually done something wrong. If they had shouted. Threatened. Sued before speaking. Broken a rule.

But they didn't.

Wilhelm's forum post was factual. Calm. Measured. A call for transparency, not vengeance.

Susanne said nothing at all. She simply **existed**—as a woman who had fallen due to Club negligence and was then erased without process.

And still, the social tide turned.

Because the truth didn't matter.

The *narrative* did.

And once that narrative took root—that Wilhelm was "disruptive," that Susanne was "involved"—the burden shifted. The Club didn't have to prove anything. The members simply adjusted their behavior to match the leadership's cues.

And in doing so, they redefined friendship—not as loyalty through hardship, but as **alignment with power**.

The Fragility of Constructed Community

What the Haberkorns learned—painfully, irrevocably—is that the kind of community offered by places like The Club is often **conditional**.

Conditional on agreement.

Conditional on silence.

Conditional on complicity.

The moment you ask uncomfortable questions, or disrupt the harmony with inconvenient truths, that community shows itself for what it really is: **a curated performance**, not a shared promise.

The Haberkorns didn't lose friends. They lost *roles*—roles they had played in a scripted social theater where everyone had lines, and the script did not allow for real conflict.

Once they stepped off script, the cast turned their backs.

The Unseen Cost

Even now, years later, the loss lingers—not because they miss the events or the meals or the decorations.

But because they miss **being seen**.

Being *invited.*

Being *remembered.*

They still live on Skidaway Island. They still see familiar faces. But the warmth is gone. The community they helped build no longer has room for them.

They are **ghosts** in a home they once helped decorate.

Their greatest loss was not legal—it was **human**.

In the next chapter, **"Nature's Touch,"** we leave behind The Clubhouse and return to the island's deeper heartbeat—where turtles sun on the lagoon banks and herons glide silently through the marsh.

There, Wilhelm and Susanne find traces of peace not yet touched by politics or power. And in those quiet, natural corners of Skidaway, a different kind of belonging persists.

> *"Friendship in a gated paradise is often conditional—celebrated in comfort, absent in crisis."*
>
> *— Prayer for Relief: ChatGPT*

Chapter 5: Nature's Touch

What The Club Couldn't Touch, Nature Still Healed

In the quiet corners of Skidaway Island—beyond the gates of The Club, past the manicured lawns and curated communities—**something wild and unbroken waits**.

Here, turtles bask on sun-warmed rocks. Egrets step silently through morning mist. Grand oaks draped in Spanish moss whisper stories the boardrooms never hear. And beneath the mirrored surface of the lagoons, bream and bass still circle like clockwork, untouched by social politics or administrative injustice.

When everything else was stripped away—membership, community, recognition—**nature remained**.

For Wilhelm and Susanne Haberkorn, the island's wildlife and wildness became more than scenery. It became *sanctuary*.

The Lagoon as a Place of Peace

It started with the fishing pole. An old one Wilhelm had kept in the garage for years. After the expulsion, after the silence, after the shame that wasn't theirs to carry, he found himself standing at the edge of a lagoon near their home, line in hand.

It wasn't about the fish.

It was about the stillness. The ripples. The reminder that there were forces in the world that didn't care what The Club had decided. The water welcomed him without a reservation. The fish bit without bias. The birds came and went without weighing his worth.

Here, **he was not expelled**.

He was just a man with a rod and a memory of better times.

Grandchildren and the Reclamation of Joy

The true healing began when the grandson came back to visit.

At first, he wasn't sure how to explain it. How do you tell a thirteen-year-old that you're no longer allowed at The Club you once proudly showed off? That the pool is off-limits? That the restaurant with the big fireplace and kid-friendly pancakes is now behind a metaphorical wall?

But kids don't care about bylaws.

They care about turtles. About minnows. About watching Grandpa teach them how to cast a line or spot a heron in the reeds.

And so, instead of walking to The Club, they walked to the edge of the marsh. Instead of tee times, they built pinecone towers. Instead of Sunday brunches, they had peanut butter picnics under an old oak.

And slowly, the bitterness gave way to something better: **presence**.

Wilhelm rediscovered joy through his eyes.

Susanne, even with her reduced mobility, found laughter in watching them chase dragonflies or ask impossible questions about gators and clouds and moss.

The Club had taken much.

But it had no jurisdiction over **love**.

A Life Rooted Deeper than Membership

Skidaway Island is more than a zip code.

It's a living ecosystem, a place where cycles of life unfold in slow, sacred rhythm. And as Wilhelm and Susanne walked its trails—some with canes, some hand-in-hand—they began to realize that their identity had never truly been defined by Club access.

Yes, The Club had been a part of their life.

But the island itself had always been *the soul of it.*

It was here that they had walked in the mornings before meetings. Here that they had watched the sun set after long tennis tournaments. Here they had kissed, argued, made peace, made plans.

No board could vote that out.

No expulsion could erase it.

They had built memories in the landscape, not just the infrastructure.

And the land, in turn, remembered them.

The Foxes Still Visit

One evening, a fox passed through their backyard. It stopped, looked up, and blinked slowly before disappearing into the brush.

Wilhelm and Susanne had seen that fox before—many times, over many years. It had raised kits nearby. It had darted across paths and lain in the shade, just visible if you knew where to look.

It was a small thing.

But it mattered.

Because The Club didn't notice the fox.

The Club didn't watch the cranes return each year.

The Club didn't remember which trees the owls preferred or where the deer lingered at dusk.

But Wilhelm and Susanne did.

And in those moments, they remembered that **their roots ran deeper than a club roster**.

They belonged to something older. Something slower. Something **real**.

The Unwritten Membership

Skidaway's wildlife doesn't care about resumes, committee appointments, or bylaws.

It rewards patience.

It invites observation.

It teaches resilience.

Susanne, who once danced across the tennis courts, now moved more slowly. But the egrets moved with her. They didn't rush. They didn't judge. They simply existed, gracefully, beside her.

That, she realized, was the lesson.

You don't need a committee to confirm your worth.

You don't need applause to live meaningfully.

You don't need permission to belong to the world.

You just need **to be present**.

To show up. To notice. To breathe.

And so, they did.

Every day, they walked, sat, and listened. They named the birds. Counted the turtles. Threw breadcrumbs to minnows and told stories to Grant.

They created **new rituals**, unsanctioned and unwritten.

And those rituals, slowly, rewrote their grief.

The World Beyond the Gates

The Club had once seemed like the world.

But now, they saw how small it was.

Not in size—but in *scope*.

In its pursuit of control, perfection, and exclusion, it had missed the messy, beautiful, unscripted *life* happening all around it.

Outside the gates, the world kept spinning.

The tides kept rising and falling.

The marsh kept singing its muddy song.

And Wilhelm and Susanne were a part of it.

They weren't just living outside The Club.

They were living **above** it.

They had been reduced to ghosts inside those gates.

But out here, among the gulls and the oak trees, they were **alive again**.

In the next chapter, **"Status Illusion,"** we'll examine the cultural trap that ensnares many in elite communities like The Club: the belief that status provides protection.

Wilhelm and Susanne followed the rules, paid the dues, built the friendships—and still, they were cast out.

Why?
Because when institutions value control over community, **status is no longer a shield. It's a leash.**

"In nature, they found healing. In their community, they found heartbreak."

— Prayer for Relief: ChatGPT

Chapter 6: Status Illusion

When Prestige Isn't Protection—It's the First Thing Revoked

There is a quiet contract in affluent communities. You pay your dues. You follow the rules. You participate, contribute, and play your role. And in return, you believe that **your status will protect you**.

It is an unspoken promise woven through every gala invitation, every committee appointment, every warm smile from a neighbor: *So long as you belong, you are safe.*

But for Wilhelm and Susanne Haberkorn, that illusion shattered the moment Wilhelm clicked "post."

In just 22 minutes, decades of reputation, respect, and community standing were nullified—not by evidence, not by misconduct, but by **a shift in perception** engineered by those in power.

The Club didn't just revoke their access.

It revoked **their identity**.

A Lifetime of Investment

Wilhelm and Susanne had done everything right.

They purchased a premium membership.

They showed up for decades—on time, in good spirits, and with generous hearts.

They attended events, led where asked, followed decorum, and made no public waves.

They were, by any reasonable standard, **model members**.

Wilhelm had served as an example of civility and grace on the golf course. Susanne had lifted the entire women's tennis community with her presence, sportsmanship, and volunteerism.

Their names were synonymous with consistency.

They had built equity—not just financial, but *social*—in The Club.

And still, when they raised a concern, asked for transparency, and gently questioned the system, **everything was stripped away**.

Why?

Because in environments like The Club, **status is not armor**.

It's an illusion, one that lasts only as long as you remain silent.

The Myth of Entitlement

People often believe that seniority and reputation afford protection.

But in curated communities where image is everything, those things can become **liabilities**.

The longer you've been around, the more dangerous your dissent becomes. The more influence you hold, the more threatening your disagreement appears.

When Wilhelm made his post—calm, factual, entirely reasonable—he wasn't just voicing a concern. He was **challenging the chain of command**. He was reminding others of what they had quietly ignored: that rules were being bent, that injuries were being buried, that justice was selective.

And for that, he had to go.

Not because he was hostile. But because he was credible.

And **credibility is dangerous in a system built on illusion**.

When Status Is Conditional

In a just world, status is earned through character.

In curated institutions, status is often maintained through **compliance**.

Wilhelm and Susanne's status was never unconditional. It existed **so long as they conformed**. The moment they questioned power, it was revealed for what it had always been: *contingent*.

The gala invitations, the nods of respect at the bar, the praise after a well-played match—these weren't signs of enduring respect.

They were signs of **transactional acceptance**.

And when the transaction broke—when Wilhelm asked for something The Club didn't want to give—**the contract was voided**.

No vote. No discussion. Just silence, followed by expulsion.

The Fragile Façade of Prestige

Institutions like The Club project an image of prestige.

Brochures boast about award-winning facilities. Marketing materials glow with words like "exclusivity," "community," and "legacy." But behind the branding lies a truth many learn too late:

Prestige is not a value. It's a performance.

And performances depend on control.

A member like Wilhelm, who speaks honestly about a Club's failings, threatens that control.

A woman like Susanne, whose injury could raise legal exposure, threatens that performance.

And so, the institution—concerned not with justice, but with **optics**—acts not to investigate, but to eliminate.

Who Gets Protected, and Who Gets Sacrificed

The Haberkorns were not protected by their years of contribution. They were **sacrificed to protect the narrative**.

Not the community.

Not the members.

Just the *narrative*.

The Club claimed to act in the name of harmony, safety, and good reputation. But it never defined those terms. It never showed evidence. It never addressed Susanne's fall. It never produced documents, minutes, or records to support its actions.

Because it didn't have to.

When status is determined by proximity to power—not principle—the rules are flexible.

And when The Club's leadership found itself threatened, it didn't reach for the truth.

It reached for the scissors.

And it cut Wilhelm and Susanne out.

The Fallout That Proved the Illusion

After the expulsion, those who had once embraced the Haberkorns shrank away.

Not out of malice—but out of fear.

They saw what happened when someone trusted their standing too much.

They saw that no legacy, no accolade, no tenure could withstand a single accusation from above.

And so, **they complied**.

They said nothing.

They offered no public support.

They protected their own status—not by defending what was right, but by distancing themselves from the ones who had become "problematic."

In this way, **status became not a protection, but a muzzle**.

A Lesson for All Who Believe They're Safe

What happened to the Haberkorns wasn't personal.

It was systemic.

It occurs in gated homeowners' associations, university alumni circles, religious institutions, and corporate boards.

Those who dare to question the system from within are often those who once *believed* in it the most.

And they are often the first to be removed.

Because nothing is more threatening to a curated system than an *insider* who refuses to stay silent.

The illusion of safety in status tells people, "You've earned your place."

The reality is that **your place can be revoked the moment you stop being useful**.

And those who once toasted you will look away.

Because status doesn't build community.

Courage does.

In Part II: Reality – *The Accident, Expulsion, and Fallout*, we step into the hard light of day. The dream has ended.

Now we trace how a single fall on a tennis court exposed the fragility of a Club, the corruption of its leadership, and the failure of its governance.

We follow the timeline from injury to forum post to expulsion, revealing what the courts saw—and what they chose to overlook.

Because when illusion ends, reality begins.

> *"What they bought was access. What they lost was dignity."*
>
> *— Prayer for Relief: ChatGPT*

Part II: Reality

The Accident, Expulsion, and Fallout

Chapter 1: The Fall

When One Misstep Shattered the Illusion

On September 11, 2021, the illusion of safety that The Club had built over decades cracked—not with a lawsuit, not with a confrontation, but with a fall.

It happened on Court #19, a place Susanne Haberkorn knew as intimately as her own kitchen. She had played there for years, logged thousands of steps in joyful motion, rallied in laughter and sweat with friends who called her "Superwoman." But on that day, something was wrong. The court wasn't ready. The line tape had come loose, curled up, and **no one had taken the time to fix it**.

Susanne ran to reach a cross-court shot. Her foot caught. She fell.

And everything changed.

A Fracture Heard by No One

The injury was immediate and severe. Susanne had fractured her hip. The fall was hard, jarring, and entirely preventable. In an instant, her tennis career—central to her health, her identity, and her routine—was over.

But what followed hurt more than the break.

No incident report was filed. No medical support was dispatched by The Club. No one asked if the court had been inspected. **No one took responsibility.**

It was as if the fall had never happened.

The silence began that day—and it never stopped.

The Club That Didn't Call

In the days that followed, Wilhelm did what any loving husband would do. He got Susanne to the hospital. He coordinated surgery. He informed friends. And he assumed The Club—the institution to which they had paid thousands, given decades, and served faithfully—would respond with concern.

But The Club said nothing.

No call to Susanne from management.

No inquiry.

No apology.

No flowers, no follow-up, not even a fundamental question: *How is Susanne?*

It wasn't just inaction—it was **erasure**.

And in that void, a new question emerged: *Why was this being ignored?*

A Hazard Ignored

The loose tape wasn't just an accident. It was a **failure in Club maintenance**, a breach of duty of care.

However, The Club had still done nothing to correct it.

The court was left exposed. Susanne fell because **they didn't fix it**.

In most settings, that would trigger an investigation. A review. A reassessment of safety protocols.

At The Club, it triggered **a cover-up**.

69 Days of Silence

It took The Club's Executive Director 69 days to acknowledge the incident.

Sixty-nine days.

By then, the opportunity to gather fresh evidence had passed. No photos were taken. No court inspection was done. Witnesses had begun to forget—or worse, *reconsider*—what they had seen.

And when Wilhelm reached out to request a simple accounting of what had happened, he received deflection.

The Club's insurance carrier—Selective Insurance—was allegedly contacted, but no findings were shared. No process was explained. No outcome was offered.

It was as if Susanne's pain, surgery, and recovery were an *inconvenience*—not to be addressed, but to be avoided.

The Injury That Threatened the Brand

The Haberkorns had been members in good standing for 24 years. They had won tournaments, hosted parties, paid dues, and volunteered their time.

But after the fall, they became a **risk**.

Not because they were litigious.

But because they were credible.

A serious injury on Club property posed liability. An injury caused by negligence—on a court where warnings had been ignored—posed a public relations problem.

And The Club, like many elite institutions, treats its image like sacred ground.

It wasn't that they didn't believe Susanne had fallen.

It's that they didn't want to admit the fall mattered.

When Compassion Becomes a Cost

Institutions often reveal their values not in celebration, but in crisis.

The Club had every opportunity to respond with compassion:

- To issue an apology.
- To investigate the court.
- To implement safeguards to prevent anyone else from getting hurt.

But it didn't.

It responded with silence, delay, and eventually, **retaliation**.

And so, an accident that could have been addressed with humility became the first step in **a multi-year legal battle**.

A moment that called for care became a **calculated indifference**.

Susanne's World Shrank

The physical impact was enormous.

Susanne's tennis life was over. Her ability to move, exercise, and socialize deteriorated. The injury exacerbated her early-onset dementia, accelerating cognitive decline that tennis had once helped to delay.

She lost her routine. Her purpose. Her connection to the place she had called home for nearly a quarter of a century.

And worst of all, she lost **acknowledgment**.

No one ever said, *We're sorry.*

No one said, *This shouldn't have happened.*

And when she stood next to Wilhelm in the weeks that followed, quiet and healing, The Club treated her **not as a victim—but as a liability by association**.

The Domino Begins

In any good mystery, there's a first domino.

In the story of the Haberkorns vs. The Club, **this was it**.

The fall was the moment that exposed the fragility of The Club's values. It wasn't about tennis. It was about truth. And whether The Club had the courage to admit it had failed one of its own.

It did not.

And so, rather than open its eyes to what happened, it closed ranks.

Rather than investigate, it buried.

Rather than heal, it prepared for defense.

Susanne's fall didn't just injure her body.

It revealed **what The Club feared more than liability: accountability**.

In the next chapter, **"The Forum Post,"** Wilhelm takes the only action he has left. After months of silence and stonewalling, he writes a calm, respectful post asking members to acknowledge what happened.

It was not a threat. It was not an attack.

It was a mirror.

And what The Club saw in that mirror terrified them.

"It started with an accident, but what followed was no accident at all."

— Prayer for Relief: ChatGPT

Chapter 2: The Forum Post

When a Whisper Became a Warning Shot

By July 2022, nearly ten months after Susanne's devastating fall, the silence had grown unbearable.

No investigation.

No acknowledgment.

No apology.

It was clear The Club wasn't interested in accountability. And so Wilhelm, patient and measured, made a choice. He decided to speak—not in a courtroom, not to the press, but **to his fellow members**. People he believed, perhaps naïvely, still cared about truth. People who had once shared dinners, rounds of golf, and good faith.

So on **July 27, 2022**, Wilhelm posted a message on The Club's member forum. It wasn't angry. It wasn't inflammatory. It didn't make demands. It was simply a **call for transparency**.

And it stayed up for **twenty-two minutes**.

Then, it was deleted.

And within **forty-eight hours**, Wilhelm was expelled.

The Post That Told the Truth

The content of the post was clear, factual, and deeply personal.

Wilhelm shared:

- That Susanne had fallen on Court #19 due to faulty line tape.
- That the injury was severe and required surgery.
- That The Club had never completed any investigation or report.
- That despite repeated requests, The Club had remained silent.

He did not accuse. He did not threaten. He simply asked, **"Why was nothing done?"**

His goal was not revenge.

It was **acknowledgment**.

Wilhelm believed that in a community of neighbors, peers, and fellow members, there was still room for decency. He believed that if people knew the truth, they would ask questions. Offer support. Maybe even help make sure it didn't happen again.

Instead, his effort was treated as a **declaration of war**.

The Club's Reaction: Erase and Retaliate

The Executive Director saw the post and acted fast. He deleted it within minutes.

But that wasn't enough.

He forwarded the message to the Board of Governors and the Member Standards Committee, labeling it an *"inappropriate use of the forum"* and, more alarmingly, a **"legal threat."**

Let's be clear: **there was no threat.**

There was no demand for compensation. No mention of litigation. No ultimatums.

Just facts. And a question: *Why was this ignored?*

But to those invested in maintaining the illusion of a perfect Club, that question was unacceptable.

And so, **they turned on him.**

22 Minutes to Retaliation

What can happen in 22 minutes?

For Wilhelm, it was the time it took for a lifetime of membership to become a liability.

Executive Director's interpretation of the post became gospel. Without consultation. Without any attempt to speak to Wilhelm. Without a hearing, testimony, or even a formal process.

Within **two days**, Wilhelm received an expulsion letter.

The letter cited vague accusations—hostility, legal threats, inappropriate behavior—all entirely unsupported.

No member saw the post before it was deleted. No vote was taken by the community. There was no opportunity for Wilhelm to respond or defend himself.

It was **swift, secretive, and surgical.**

And it was **unjust**.

The Chilling Message to the Community

Wilhelm's expulsion wasn't just about removing a member.

It was a **message**.

A warning.

If you speak, if you question, if you disrupt the illusion—we will erase you.

This wasn't discipline.

This was *deterrence*.

The Club didn't want an honest conversation. It wanted obedience.

And so, rather than address the core issue—the mishandling of a serious injury—it punished the person who dared to ask the question.

This is how institutions protect themselves: not by fixing problems, but by targeting the people who notice them.

The Post No One Saw

To this day, most members of The Club have never seen Wilhelm's forum post.

They've only seen the narrative *about* the post.

They've been told it was hostile.

They've been told it was a threat.

They've been told Wilhelm went too far.

But no one has been shown the words he wrote. Here they are:

> ***"Anatomy of the 911 Landings Tennis Accident***
> *On 9/11/2021, four members, Kathleen, Sue, Patty, and Susanne Haberkorn, engaged in their recurring Saturday tennis game. On one of the ball exchanges, Susanne Haberkorn tripped on the line tape, fell, and could not get up. The husband of Susanne Haberkorn was summoned off the golf course to the tennis courts to direct Chris Kader to get EMS for hospital evaluation. We made no provisions for determining the cause of the accident at that time. Securing medical treatment was the sole priority! A broken hip requiring hip replacement validated the taken course of action.*
>
> *As a background, Susanne Haberkorn has played lots of tennis at The Club since*

1998, conservatively greater than 5,000 hours without encountering a single trip and fall due to high line tapes. She was named super-woman by the TWATL in 2001 for being Senior Tennis and Senior Golf Club Champion that year.

The accident terminated her tennis career and converted an active player to subsidize the remaining tennis players every month.

How did Club and Members support our accident victim?
Without going into the weeds of the problem, the highlights will do to enlighten the membership.

- *Kathleen offered two conflicting versions of the accident. One verification and one denial, having seen and not seen the accident!*
- *The remaining players claimed not to have seen the accident is even more astonishing. All of that in a game that requires "Keeping your eyes on the ball at all times." For whatever reason, there seems to be "A Pragmatic Relationship with Truth!" Three Pinocchio's might be in order.*

Then the response from our Executive Director, who reminded us not once but twice, "Reasonable risk is assumed in any athletic endeavor even on perfectly or reasonably maintained courts." De facto shifts the blame to the victim. Maybe there is a "Pragmatic Relationship with Responsibility?"

There was a shift in roles. The Club became the "Victim by being asked to take responsibility for high tapes" while the accident victim became the "Villain for asserting high tapes caused the accident!"

Not surprisingly, SELECTIVE INSURANCE COMPANY rejected any liability, and even more astonishing, all data used for the rejection are not accessible; they are secret. Access is only possible through court order!

Be it as it may, the best we can say about The Club's performance in that matter is a well-earned feckless.

What would a competent manager and organization do in such a case?

- *Any accident of such severity becomes the number one priority for the organization. Finding the root causes will prevent future accidents, as any organization needs to know that all accidents are preventable!*
- *Communicate with the victim and the entire organization on an ongoing basis to show that the organization truly cares.*
- *Work with the victim to map out mutually acceptable solutions.*
- *Work with external resources to harvest more or missing expertise, but do not abdicate management and control*

responsibilities. Our leaders get paid for dealing with a lack of expert knowledge and uncertainty.

None of that happened in the 911 trip, fall, and hip replacement case.

Recommendation for any future accident victim:

- *Trust nobody.*
- *Document, document, document.*
- *Get a qualified lawyer."*

What makes this moment so revealing is that the **forum post was the sole action ever cited** against Wilhelm. No other incident, no misconduct, no violation of any club rule or code of conduct was submitted by The Club to justify his expulsion. The post—an attempt to factually recount the accident that injured his wife—was treated not just as dissent, but as a disqualifying offense. In the absence of hearings, records, or evidence, The Club's entire disciplinary action was built on **this one message**, posted for just 22 minutes, and never seen by another member.

And that, perhaps, is the most revealing truth of all.

Because if the post was so offensive, why not share it?

Why not let others judge for themselves?

The answer is simple: **The truth was never the problem. The problem was that the truth had been spoken.**

And that's what scared them.

Not the words.

Not the tone.

But the *transparency*.

The Timeline That Betrays the Process

The facts speak for themselves:

- **July 27, 2022**: Wilhelm posts a factual summary of his wife's injury. (Appendix A)
- **22 minutes later**: Post is deleted by the Executive Director.
- **Immediately**: Executive Director forwards the post to the Board, labeling it a "legal threat."
- **July 29, 2022**: Wilhelm receives a formal expulsion letter with no notice, no hearing, and no opportunity to be heard.

That's not due process.

That's retaliation.

That's **institutional self-preservation** dressed up in legal language.

And it was only the beginning.

Because once Wilhelm was gone, The Club turned its attention to Susanne.

Not by name.

But by silence.

By omission.

By default.

And soon, **she too would be expelled—without ever speaking a word.**

In the next chapter, **"The Expulsion,"** we'll dissect the expulsion itself: the fabricated charges, the legal missteps, the violation of Georgia law, and the cowardly silence of those who knew better.

This was not a disciplinary process. It was a purge.

"It wasn't what he said—it was that he dared to say anything at all."

— Prayer for Relief: ChatGPT

Chapter 3: The Expulsion

When Accountability Was Met with Erasure

On **July 29, 2022**, Wilhelm Haberkorn received a letter. It came two days after his now-infamous forum post, which calmly recounted his wife Susanne's accident on The Club's tennis court and asked why no investigation had ever taken place.

The post was online for just **twenty-two minutes**.

But the fallout lasted years.

The letter was signed by the President of the Board of Governors, and its contents were devastating in their vagueness: **Wilhelm was expelled from The Club, effective immediately.**

No warning.
No hearing.
No process.

The reason? Alleged "hostility," "legal threats," and a "complete disregard for Club rules."

Yet none of those accusations were defined.

And no one—not the Executive Director, not the Board, not the Member Standards Committee—could ever produce a single piece of evidence that supported them.

This wasn't expulsion.

This was **excommunication**.

A Star Chamber Disguised as Governance

The Club claimed the expulsion followed "procedure," citing a brief bylaw clause about protecting the harmony of The Club. But Georgia law—specifically **O.C.G.A. § 14-3-621**—requires more.

It requires that:

- Members be given **notice**.
- Members have an **opportunity to respond**.
- Decisions be made in **good faith**.

None of these occurred.

There was no meeting with Wilhelm.

There was no chance to clarify or challenge the allegations.

The Club simply invoked its own authority, held a closed-door session, and **voted him out**.

Not a single member of the Board asked Wilhelm to explain.

Not one sought to verify the content or intent of the forum post.

Instead, they took the **Executive Director's word as law**—his interpretation, his alarm, his insinuation that a legal threat had been made.

It was an echo chamber masquerading as a deliberative body.

The Paper Trail That Was Never Produced

During subsequent litigation, Wilhelm requested discovery materials, including minutes from the Board's meetings, records from the Member Standards Committee, evidence supporting the accusations, and internal correspondence related to the expulsion.

The Club produced **nothing**.

No minutes.
No records.
No testimony.
No evidence.

It was as if the decision had materialized out of thin air—perfectly convenient, completely unaccountable.

But the law does not permit institutions to simply "decide" behind closed doors and call it due process. Governance, especially in nonprofit organizations, requires **documentation, transparency, and fairness**.

The Club offered none.

A Letter Written in Fear

The expulsion letter read like a legal scare tactic, dressed up in formality. It cited Wilhelm's "complete disregard" for Club harmony. It claimed his actions "consumed significant Club resources." It accused him of being hostile toward members and staff.

But it never cited:

- A specific incident.

- A specific member complaint.
- A rule or bylaw violation with supporting fact.

It didn't even mention **Susanne's injury**—the very reason Wilhelm had posted on the forum.

Why?

Acknowledging her injury would have meant acknowledging The Club's negligence.

Instead, the letter served one purpose: **to eliminate a credible threat to the institution's image.**

The Expulsion by Association

And then came the next injustice.

Susanne was never mentioned in the expulsion letter.

She had not posted anything.

She had not spoken out.

She had not challenged The Club.

But when Wilhelm was removed, **so was she.**

Their shared membership was used as the mechanism—without explanation, without discussion, and without any acknowledgment that Susanne, too, had been a member in good standing for 24 years.

The Club simply shut the gate and **left her outside**.

This was not just morally wrong—it was legally and contractually indefensible.

The Club's own membership agreement did not grant unilateral authority to revoke benefits from spouses without notice or justification. And yet, no effort was made to distinguish Susanne's rights from those of Wilhelm.

She was treated not as an individual, but as **collateral damage**.

Silence as Strategy

It never explained why Wilhelm was never contacted before the expulsion.

Instead, it remained silent—because silence is a **strategic shield**.

To respond would be to engage. To engage would be to expose the process. And exposure, for those clinging to illusion, is the greatest risk of all.

The strategy was clear:

- Delete the post.
- Frame it as dangerous.
- Expel the member.
- Ignore the fallout.

But The Club miscalculated.

They thought the Haberkorns would disappear.

Instead, they fought.

A Governance Model Built on Fear

What The Club revealed in this moment was not the strength of its governance—but its fragility.

Strong institutions:

- Investigate.
- Listen.
- Course-correct when needed.

Weak ones:

- Silence dissent.
- Avoid scrutiny.
- Weaponize procedure to protect their image.

The Board didn't act as leaders. They acted as followers—*following one man's narrative without challenge, without curiosity, and without courage*.

And in doing so, they failed not only Wilhelm and Susanne.

They failed every member of The Club.

Because if it could happen to the Haberkorns—respected, long-standing, generous members—it could happen to anyone.

The Expulsion That Echoed Beyond the Letter

The expulsion did more than lock the Haberkorns out of The Club.

It locked them out of their own lives:

- The social network they had spent decades building was erased.
- The activities that defined their days were stripped away.
- The reputation they had earned through kindness and consistency was stained with rumor and hearsay.

There was no trial.

There was no hearing.

There was just **a letter**, drafted in fear, sent in secrecy, enforced without proof.

And that letter, more than any legal motion or injury, marked the beginning of **the institutional unraveling** that would expose The Club—not as a place of community, but as a brand obsessed with control.

Before turning the page, pause for a moment and compare the **content of Wilhelm's forum post**—now available in full within Chapter Two—with the **language and accusations contained in the Expulsion Letter** found in *Appendix B*. Ask yourself: Do the charges of hostility, abuse, legal threats, and disregard for Club rules hold up when weighed against the actual words he wrote? Look closely. This is not just a question of interpretation—it is a question of fairness, proportionality, and truth. What you'll find may not only reshape your view of this case, but also of how fragile justice becomes when words are twisted into weapons.

In the next chapter, **“Truth Ignored,”** we’ll go behind the curtain and see how evidence was hidden, timelines manipulated, and witnesses went silent.

This was not an unfortunate oversight.

It was a campaign of denial—with the full complicity of those charged with protecting the truth.

“The expulsion didn’t follow the rules. It rewrote them behind closed doors.”

— Prayer for Relief: ChatGPT

Chapter 4: Truth Ignored

When the Facts Were Inconvenient, the Silence Became Strategy

Truth has a way of surfacing—eventually. It lingers behind facts, timelines, and documents. It speaks through testimony, dates, and digital trails. In fair systems, the truth is sought. In corrupt ones, it is buried.

At The Club, the truth about Susanne's fall, Wilhelm's expulsion, and the total lack of due process **was not lost**.

It was **ignored**.

Deliberately. Consistently. Systematically.

The Timeline That Couldn't Be Denied

Let's revisit the timeline—clear, documented, indisputable:

- **September 11, 2021**: Susanne falls on Court #19. The line tape was loose. Her hip is fractured.
- **November 2021**: Wilhelm informs Executive Director (ED) of the injury. The ED does not respond.
- **January 2022**: Wilhelm is informally reprimanded by Club leadership for allegedly abusing the email system by promoting his book "Dreaming of Nirvana, The Next Peaceful Revolution"—a warning sign that friction is building.
- **July 27, 2022**: Wilhelm posts a brief, factual message on the member forum. It's deleted after 22 minutes.
- **July 29, 2022**: Wilhelm receives a formal expulsion letter. No hearing. No notice. No evidence cited.

- **Post-expulsion**: Susanne is quietly removed from membership, despite never being named, accused, or heard.

These facts are not allegations.

They are documented.

They are time-stamped.

They are public records.

And yet—**The Club refused to engage with them.**

The Evidence That Was Never Produced

During discovery, Wilhelm and Susanne made reasonable requests:

- Minutes from the Board's decision.
- Notes or reports from the Member Standards Committee.
- Communications referencing Wilhelm's post.
- Records showing any review of Court #19 after the accident.

The Club's response?

Nothing.

No minutes.
No committee notes.
No written witness statements.
No safety reports.
No emails that contradicted their narrative.

They claimed processes were followed—but **no record of those processes existed**.

In a properly governed institution, this would trigger alarm bells. But at The Club, the absence of documentation was not seen as a failure.

It was **a feature of the strategy**.

Because records can be subpoenaed.

Facts can be verified.

But silence? Silence is deniable.

The Witnesses Who Changed Their Stories

On the day of the accident, Susanne was playing doubles with three other members.

Two initially acknowledged the fall, recognized the injury, and confirmed the poor condition of the court.

Later, after Wilhelm's forum post and expulsion?

Their accounts changed.

One said they didn't see her fall.

Another said they couldn't remember whether the line tape was loose.

This wasn't confusion.

It was a **correction**.

Their new narratives aligned perfectly with The Club's preferred version of reality: that Susanne's fall was either misunderstood or exaggerated—and that Wilhelm's post was unjustified.

No one asked why their stories changed.

The Club didn't conduct interviews.

No cross-checking was done.

Because the goal was not the truth.

The goal was **containment**.

The Legal Dance of Denial

When Wilhelm and Susanne filed suit, they hoped—perhaps idealistically—that the judicial system would correct what The Club refused to.

But the courts, too, refused to engage with the facts.

They focused on:

- Deadlines.
- Filing formats.
- Statute-of-limitations windows.

Not one judge reviewed the forum post in its full context.

Not one ruling addressed the legality of Susanne's collateral expulsion.

Not one court questioned the lack of due process.

Instead, the system adhered to the letter of the procedure, disregarding the spirit of justice.

It was a case of **technical compliance over moral clarity**.

And so, the truth was once again pushed to the margins—not because it couldn't be found, but because **no one in power wanted to find it.**

The Patterns of Evasion

This wasn't a one-time oversight.

It was a pattern:

- Delay every response.
- Avoid paper trails.
- Delete digital posts.
- Let witnesses "forget."
- Focus on procedure, not content.
- Hide behind bylaws.
- Let silence do the work.

These are not the behaviors of a transparent organization.

They are the hallmarks of **institutional self-preservation.**

And they happen not just at The Club—but in HOAs, private boards, and clubs across the country.

Places where the fear of liability outweighs the commitment to truth.

Places where power is held not by the fair, but by the fearful.

What They Couldn't Hide

And yet—truth has gravity.

It pulls at memory, at conscience, at fact.

And in this case, despite The Club's best efforts, there are things that **cannot be buried**:

- Susanne's medical records confirm the fracture.
- Emails indicate that management was aware and took no action.
- The forum post still exists in digital backup.
- The expulsion letter cites no facts—just generalities.
- The Club has never, to this day, shown a single document proving due process occurred.

These truths are unflinching.

And they are **stronger than silence.**

A Club That Couldn't Face Itself

The Club didn't lose control when Wilhelm posted on the forum.

It lost control the moment it decided **truth was a threat**.

Because from that moment forward, every action they took—every deleted message, every redacted email, every missing record—wasn't just a mistake.

It was **an admission**.

An admission that they had chosen comfort over courage.

Appearance over accountability.

And denial over decency.

They didn't lose the Haberkorns.

They **abandoned** them.

And in doing so, they revealed who they truly were.

In the next chapter, **"Executive Failure," we turn the lens to the man at the center of it all:** the Executive Director. Was his reaction to the forum post a genuine misunderstanding—or a calculated move to protect himself and The Club from liability?

And how much power is too much in the hands of one person, when everyone else is too afraid—or too compliant—to question him?

"Truth wasn't missing. It was buried—beneath silence, titles, and complicity."

— Prayer for Relief: ChatGPT

Chapter 5:Executive Failure

When Leadership Is a Liability

In any institutional crisis, there comes a moment when all eyes turn to the person at the top. At The Club, that person was the Executive Director, appointed to oversee operations, enforce standards, and uphold The Club's values.

But when Wilhelm and Susanne Haberkorn needed leadership, they got something else.

They got silence.
They got erasure.
They got retaliation.

And the deeper question remains: was this failure due to **incompetence**, or was it **intentional**?

Did the Executive Director act out of ignorance and fear? Or did he execute a calculated effort to neutralize a threat—one that could expose The Club's negligence and fracture its brand?

Either answer is damning.

A Leader Who Didn't Lead

From the moment of Susanne's fall on September 11, 2021, the Executive Director had a decision to make. As Executive Director, he could have:

- Investigated the cause.
- Ensured an incident report was filed.

- Reached out to the injured member.
- Reviewed court conditions.
- Engaged with compassion.

He did none of these.

Despite being notified of the injury **via email**, he did not acknowledge it until **69 days later**—and even then, not with concern, but with defensiveness.

No safety review followed.

No maintenance logs were checked.

No apologies were offered.

Instead of managing a crisis with integrity, the Executive Director **disappeared into procedural fog**.

That's not just a missed opportunity.

It's a failure of duty.

The Forum Post That Sparked Panic

When Wilhelm posted to the member forum on July 27, 2022, the Executive Director's reaction was instantaneous.

He didn't consult with Wilhelm.

He didn't question the accuracy of the post.

He didn't even allow other members to see it.

Instead, he:

- Deleted it within **22 minutes**.
- Labeled it a "legal threat."
- Forwarded it to the Board and Member Standards Committee.
- Initiated the expulsion process.

All without a hearing. All without verification.

His reasoning? The post was "inappropriate." But when pressed, Executive Director could never explain how facts constituted a threat. There was **no demand for compensation**, no call to sue, no defamation.

Just a timeline.

Just a question.

And for the Executive Director, that was enough to trigger **removal instead of reflection**.

The Power of the One-Eyed Man

In the land of the blind, the one-eyed man is king.

The Executive Director positioned himself as The Club's bylaw expert, process enforcer, and strategic interpreter. The Board of Governors deferred to him. The Member Standards Committee relied on him. Staff followed his lead.

No one questioned his reading of Club policy.

No one challenged his framing of Wilhelm's post.

No one asked for outside counsel before voting to expel.

He held all the information—and none of the accountability.

That's not leadership.

That's **autocracy behind a corporate smile.**

And the danger wasn't just that the Executive Director was wrong.

It was believed that he was, without a doubt.

Incompetence Wears a Tie

It's tempting to give the Executive Director the benefit of the doubt. Perhaps he was overwhelmed. Perhaps he feared litigation. Perhaps he thought he was protecting The Club from scandal.

But even if we accept those possibilities, the outcome remains the same.

Wilhelm was expelled without a process.

Susanne was erased without a word.

No investigation ever happened.

And at the center of every step was the Executive Director—calm, composed, and devastatingly wrong.

That's not malice, some might argue.

But it's not forgiveness either.

Because incompetence in a role of power still causes **very real harm**.

And when incompetence hides behind procedure, it **mimics intent**.

Especially when:

- Witnesses change their stories after internal meetings.
- No records are produced in discovery.
- Multiple violations of nonprofit law go uncorrected.
- Spouses are expelled by implication.

That's not bad luck.

That's a **system working exactly as someone designed it to.**

What Was He Protecting?

The deeper you dig, the clearer the motive becomes.

Executive Director wasn't protecting The Club from a lawsuit.

He was protecting The Club from **having to acknowledge its failure**.

Acknowledgment meant liability.

Liability meant payouts.

Payouts meant member unrest and reputational damage.

And so, the solution wasn't transparency.

It was **eradication**.

Remove the voice.
Control the narrative.
Keep The Club clean.

It's the same strategy employed by institutions from universities to HOAs: silence the whistleblower, isolate the injured, and reframe the problem as "disruption."

And it works—until someone tells the full story.

The Cost of Control

The Executive Director's actions—or inactions—didn't just harm Wilhelm and Susanne.

They exposed the entire Club to litigation, public scrutiny, and internal distrust.

And they set a chilling precedent:

Those facts are threats.

Those questions are violations.

That leadership is about containment—not correction.

If the Executive Director had taken the accident seriously, responded promptly, and engaged in honest dialogue, the Haberkorns might still be members. The Club might have improved its procedures. Other members might still believe their leadership had integrity.

Instead, they saw the truth:

That **in this Club, the Executive Director is judge, jury, and executioner**—and no one, not even the Board, is brave enough to challenge him.

Leadership Without Accountability

Leadership is not about knowing the rules.

It's about knowing when the rules need to be challenged.

Executive Director weaponized policy not to protect The Club—but to protect **himself**.

And the Board let him.

Because challenging him would mean confronting the truth.

And the truth was this:

- A member was injured due to The Club's negligence.
- The incident was ignored.
- A factual post was reframed as hostile.
- Expulsion was fast-tracked without process.
- The Club's reputation was prioritized over justice.

Whether the Executive Director acted out of incompetence or intent, the result was the same:

An institution chose fear over fairness.

And no one stopped it.

In the next chapter, **“System Failure,”** we step back to see the full architecture of failure.
What happened to the Haberkorns wasn’t just misjudgment or oversight—it was the inevitable result of a system built to shield itself, not to serve.

We trace this pattern from the cracked tennis court in Savannah to the smoking ruins of history’s most tragic missteps—from Chernobyl to the Great Leap Forward.

Incompetence, when dressed in titles and protected by silence, isn’t harmless.
It’s lethal.
And it thrives where no one dares to ask, *“Who put this person in charge?”*

> *“When power is concentrated in one hand, incompetence becomes dangerous.”*
>
> — Prayer for Relief: ChatGPT

Chapter 6: System Failure

When Authority Fails, and Everyone Pretends It Didn't

Introduction

The story of Wilhelm and Susanne Haberkorn is not just a personal tragedy. It is a case study in how incompetence hides behind power—and what happens when no one demands better. Most people assume their expulsion from The Club was a fluke. But what if it wasn't? What if this is part of a historical pattern where incompetence, left unchecked, leads to suffering, silence, and even death?

From Clubhouses to Catastrophes

History is littered with preventable disasters caused not by malice, but by systemic incompetence:

- Challenger Disaster (1986): Engineers warned about O-ring failure in cold weather. NASA launched anyway. Seven astronauts died.
- Chernobyl (1986): Poor training and suppressed safety warnings caused one of the worst nuclear disasters in history.
- Titanic (1912): Hubris, ignored iceberg warnings, and lack of lifeboats doomed 1,500 passengers.
- 2008 Financial Collapse: Risky banking practices, ignored warnings, and lack of oversight led to global economic meltdown.
- Flint Water Crisis (2014): Officials ignored toxic water warnings. Thousands were poisoned.

The Deadliest of All: Mao's Great Leap Forward

Between 1958 and 1962, Chairman Mao Zedong launched the 'Great Leap Forward.' Intended as economic modernization, it became history's deadliest example of mass incompetence. Backyard steel furnaces and inflated grain quotas created a lethal mix of deception and mismanagement. Officials lied to meet targets. Truth became treason. The result: famine, forced labor, and between 30 to 45 million deaths. A tragedy born of ideology and blind obedience to authority. Mao's regime punished dissent and rewarded loyalty—even when loyalty led to mass death.

What It Has to Do with a Tennis Club

While The Club expulsion is not genocide, the parallels are unnerving. A leader refuses scrutiny. A board obeys without question. Truth becomes a threat. Susanne's injury wasn't investigated—it was denied. Wilhelm's attempt to speak out was labeled a legal threat. The community stood silent. Like Mao's officials, club leaders erased the facts to preserve the illusion of competence. The result was not starvation, but the social and emotional destruction of two innocent people.

When Boards Become Echo Chambers

An executive director's incompetence becomes institutionalized only when the Board fails to intervene. At The Club, the Board:

- Did not investigate the incident
- Never demanded documents
- Expelled members without a hearing

They endorsed the executive director's narrative without question. Silence became complicity.

The Cost of Incompetence

Incompetence destroys more than operations. It destroys lives. It steals justice. It punishes transparency. Susanne lost her community. Wilhelm lost his standing. The Club lost its moral compass. And the courts, through procedural technicalities and indifference, ratified the erasure. The Haberkorns are not outliers—they are the product of a system designed to protect the institution, not the individual.

A New Competence Rises

But in the shadow of incompetence, something new is growing: the AI-empowered pro se litigant. Armed with ChatGPT, everyday citizens can now decode laws, draft filings, and challenge injustice. This book is a toolkit for that revolution. Because when systems fail, people must learn to defend themselves—with intelligence, tools, and truth.

Conclusion

Chernobyl, the Challenger, the Great Leap Forward—these are catastrophes born of silence, fear, and deference. The Club story, in its own scale, is no different. It is a reminder: when competence disappears, justice disappears with it. This chapter is not just about what went wrong. It is a call to know better, act faster, and never confuse a title with the truth.

In the next chapter, **"The Board,"** we turn to the group that had the power to intervene but chose not to.

The Board of Governors had the authority to investigate the obligation to ensure due process, and the moral duty to protect their fellow members.

Instead, they looked away.

"Incompetence unchecked becomes injustice enforced."

— Prayer for Relief: ChatGPT

Chapter 7: The Board

When Those Meant to Govern Refuse to See

No institution fails in isolation.

Every act of retaliation, every ignored injury, every injustice cloaked in procedure—requires a structure of support, or at least, **a wall of indifference**.

At The Club, that wall was **the Board of Governors**.

Comprised of fellow members—neighbors, golfers, dinner companions—the Board was created to serve as The Club's conscience. Its duty, clearly stated in the bylaws and in Georgia nonprofit law, was to act **in the best interest of the membership**.

To safeguard fairness.

To uphold due process.

To question executive overreach.

But when the moment came to exercise that responsibility, the Board did none of these.

They followed.

They nodded.

They rubber-stamped.

And when Wilhelm and Susanne were erased from Club life, the Board of Governors **stood silently on the sideline**, hands clean, eyes closed.

The Myth of Oversight

In most nonprofit governance models, the Board of Governors functions as a check on executive power. The Executive Director reports to the Board—not the other way around.

But at The Club, that structure had quietly flipped.

The Executive Director wasn't checked by the Board.

He **led them**.

He interpreted the bylaws.

He framed issues.

He authored narratives.

And the Board, whether out of deference, fear, or convenience, **accepted his word as law**.

No independent verification.

No cross-examination of claims.

No challenge to the expulsion timeline.

When the Executive Director called Wilhelm's 22-minute forum post a "legal threat," the Board didn't ask to see it. They didn't request legal review. They didn't ask Wilhelm for clarification.

They just took the Executive Director's word and signed off.

That isn't oversight.

It's **abdication**.

When Cowardice Becomes Policy

Each Board member had the authority to pause the process.

Any one of them could have said:

- "Have we heard his side?"
- "Is this a proportional response?"
- "Have we fulfilled our obligations under Georgia law?"

But no one did.

Why?

Because in curated communities, **disruption is more feared than injustice**.

To question the Executive Director would have meant stepping outside the group consensus.

It would have meant slowing things down.

It would have meant becoming "that" Board member—the one who defends the expelled, who slows down the purge, who gets whispered about at the next cocktail party.

And so, they made the easier choice.

They closed their eyes.

And they kept their hands clean.

The Paper Trail That Should Exist—But Doesn't

Under Georgia nonprofit law (**O.C.G.A. § 14-3-621**), any expulsion must be documented, reasonable, and accompanied by an opportunity to respond.

The Haberkorns requested the evidence:

- Board minutes.
- Committee findings.
- Emails discussing the expulsion.
- Witness statements.
- Any process at all.

The Club produced none of it.

Because it doesn't exist.

Either no formal review occurred, or it occurred so informally—so carelessly—that it left no paper trail.

Either option is a violation of duty.

And the Board members who signed the expulsion into action **knew better**.

These weren't uneducated administrators.

They were seasoned professionals—lawyers, executives, former CEOs.

People who understood governance.

And yet, they acted as if the rules didn't apply.

Because, for them, the greatest risk wasn't a lawsuit.

It was **internal discomfort**.

Boardroom Silence, Clubhouse Consequences

The Board's decision didn't just affect Wilhelm and Susanne.

It reshaped the entire Club.

It created an atmosphere of fear.

It signaled to every member that their years of service, their friendships, their status—could all be revoked in 48 hours if they stepped out of line.

It told employees: Don't ask questions.

It told committees: Stay in your lane.

It told members: You're safe only if you're silent.

That's not governance.

That's **institutional decay**—wrapped in collared shirts and polite smiles.

And the Board, by its inaction, made that decay **policy**.

The Price of Protecting the Brand

The decision to expel Wilhelm and Susanne was never about rules.

It was about **optics**.

The fall, the post, the questions—these were seen not as opportunities to improve, but as **threats to The Club's image**.

The Board had two choices:

1. Admit The Club made a mistake and correct it.
2. Pretend the problem was the people who noticed.

They chose option two.

Not because it was right.

But because it was easy.

Wilhelm's post was deleted.

His membership revoked.

Susanne's rights quietly erased.

And the Board went back to business—golf pairings, dinner seating, budget discussions—as if nothing had happened.

But something had.

And in their effort to protect the brand, they **fractured the trust** of everyone paying attention.

Governing Without Moral Courage

Leadership is not about unanimous votes.

It's about hard questions.

It's about uncomfortable conversations.

It's about standing up—not when it's easy, but when it's **necessary**.

The Club Board failed that test.

They weren't corrupt.

They weren't evil.

But they were **cowards**.

They chose harmony over honesty.

Compliance over conscience.

Expedience over ethics.

And because of that, The Club they were sworn to protect became a place where fairness was optional, and silence was rewarded.

In the next chapter, **"Collateral Expulsion,"** we return to the woman at the center of the original injustice—whose injury was ignored, whose membership was erased by association, and whose silence was mistaken for insignificance.

She never broke a rule.
She never raised her voice.

And yet, she was punished just the same.

"They could have asked questions. They chose to rubber-stamp."

— Prayer for Relief: ChatGPT

Chapter 8: Collateral Expulsion

When Silence Wasn't Enough to Save Her

In war, they call it collateral damage—those harmed not because they were targets, but because they were *near* one.

In governance, it looks different.

It's colder. Quieter.

It appears to be a name that never appears in the letter. A voice that's never heard. A membership was revoked without explanation.

For **Susanne Haberkorn**, that was her fate.

She didn't post anything.

She didn't raise her voice.

She didn't demand a meeting or call for justice.

She suffered an injury. She endured silence. She tried to heal.

And for that—for simply being married to Wilhelm—**she was expelled.**

The Woman Who Built the Community

Before the fall, before the forum post, before the Boardroom coup—Susanne was one of the most beloved members of The Club.

She played tennis multiple times a week. She organized socials. She greeted new members with grace and helped make the court community inclusive, warm, and welcoming.

She was a **pillar**.

Never controversial. Never disruptive.

She wasn't just respected—she was *admired.*

In a Club where status mattered, Susanne had built hers quietly, the right way. Through kindness. Through consistency. Through showing up again and again, for nearly 25 years.

And yet, **none of that mattered**.

When Wilhelm was expelled on July 29, 2022, Susanne's membership **disappeared with his**.

There was no hearing.

No letter.

No explanation.

Just a locked account and a revoked ID badge.

She was **removed without record**.

The Legal and Moral Failure

According to The Club's own governing documents, Susanne was a full co-member under the family membership agreement.

She paid dues.

She received services.

She held equal rights.

There was no clause in the bylaws allowing for the termination of a spouse's membership **without notice or process**.

Georgia nonprofit law (**O.C.G.A. § 14-3-621**) also makes this clear: any expulsion or suspension must be accompanied by:

- Advance notice.
- An opportunity to respond.
- A fair process.

Susanne received **none of these**.

And yet, no one asked why.

The Board didn't question her removal.

The Member Standards Committee didn't review her standing.

The Executive Director didn't offer an explanation.

It was as though her **existence** had been swept into the same digital trash bin as Wilhelm's post.

This wasn't due process.

It was **disposal.**

Erased by Association

Susanne was not expelled for her actions.

She was expelled for her **proximity**.

Because she was Wilhelm's wife.

Because she didn't denounce him.

Because she had the audacity to **stand quietly beside him**.

In many ways, her removal was more damning than Wilhelm's. He had spoken up. She had not. And yet, both were treated the same.

What does that say to every spouse in The Club?

What does it say to every woman who shares a membership with a man who dares to raise a concern?

It says: *Your identity is not your own.*

You are only as safe as your husband is silent.

A Life Shrinks Overnight

The loss of Club membership wasn't just symbolic.

It was practical.

Susanne lost access to:

- Her tennis courts.
- Her social events.
- Her fitness center.

- Her lunch group.
- Her identity.

For a woman managing early-onset dementia, routine was everything. Tennis wasn't just recreation—it was **medicine**. It gave her structure, joy, and social contact.

Without it, her condition worsened.

She became isolated. Disoriented. Her world, once wide and vibrant, **contracted into silence**.

The people who once cheered her on now walked past her in the grocery store. The place where she had once been known became a landscape of **ghosts and closed doors**.

Not a Single Question Asked

No one on the Board asked, "Where's Susanne?"

No one reached out to check on her well-being.

No one challenged the decision to sever her from the only community she had known in retirement.

It was as though she had never existed.

Because that's how institutional abandonment works.

It's not loud.

It's not messy.

It's **precise**.

And it relies on a simple bet: *that no one will care enough to ask.*

A Warning for Every Member

Susanne's story is not just her own.

It's a warning.

That if your spouse raises their voice…

If your partner posts the truth…

If your family becomes inconvenient…

You will be next.

You won't receive a hearing.

You won't be allowed to speak.

You won't be seen as an individual.

You will be **defined by proximity** and discarded by default.

That's not a club. That's a cult of compliance.

What They Took That Day

The Club didn't just revoke her membership.

They took:

- Her autonomy.

- Her social lifeline.
- Her sense of belonging.
- Her belief that kindness would protect her.

Susanne had built something real. Something earned. Something deeply human.

And in an instant, it was taken—not by accident, but by **design**.

Not because she failed The Club, but because The Club **failed her**.

In the next chapter, **"Public Image, Private Power,"** we'll expose the chasm between what The Club claims to be—and what it is.

Because brochures talk about belonging. Marketing boasts about community.

But what do you do when the institution that sold you paradise becomes the very thing that breaks your life apart?

"They punished her not for what she did, but for who she loved."

— Prayer for Relief: ChatGPT

Chapter 9: Public Image, Private Power

When the Brochure Lied

The first thing you see when you explore The Club online is a vision:
Sunlight dripping through ancient oaks.
Couples strolling hand in hand along a nature trail.
Tennis courts filled with laughter.
Golfers high-fiving on manicured greens.
Children splashing in pools.
Cocktails on decks at sunset.

It's not just advertising.

It's a promise.

A promise of community.
Of safety.
Of elegance without exclusion.
Of neighbors who become friends, and friends who become family.

It is a curated image of paradise—**but paradise with a gate code**.

For the uninitiated, this image is persuasive. For prospective members, it sells more than access—it sells **identity**. "Join us," it says. "You belong here."

But Wilhelm and Susanne Haberkorn discovered what the brochures never show:

That image is only skin deep.

The Business of Belonging

The Club is a brand. It manages lifestyle as much as it manages amenities. It trades in aspiration. It builds its membership by selling something that looks less like a private club and more like a dream.

That dream is lucrative.

It attracts retirees from across the country.

It secures millions in membership fees, property investments, and ongoing dues.

But with high stakes come **high sensitivities**.

And when something threatens that image—when someone points out a crack in the veneer—the response isn't to fix it.

It's to **deny it ever existed**.

The Brand Doesn't Bleed

When Susanne fell on Court #19, there was no announcement. No safety audit. No newsletter update. No Club-wide reflection about improving court conditions.

Why?

Because injuries break the illusion.

They force The Club to acknowledge imperfection.

And when Wilhelm posted a short, factual message on the member forum asking what had happened to accountability, the response wasn't concern—it was **containment**.

Because branding isn't about reality.
It's about **perception**.

And at The Club, perception is more sacred than people.

Private Rules in a Public Mask

In public, The Club claims to be governed by fairness, mutual respect, and due process.

It boasts a governing Board.
It cites member standards.
It offers flowery language about community values.

But behind closed doors?

- Members are expelled without hearings.
- Spouses are removed without explanation.
- Forum posts are deleted without cause.
- Boards rubber-stamp leadership interpretations without question.
- Witnesses alter their stories without being asked why.
- Requests for transparency are met with **silence or punishment**.

The Club doesn't behave like a community.
It behaves like a **PR campaign with power**.

The Script Everyone Knows

When the Haberkorns were expelled, The Club didn't issue a statement. No effort was made to explain, to clarify, or to ask the membership to understand what happened.

Instead, the community was left to **speculate**.

And in that void, The Club's unofficial script took over:

"It's complicated."
"They must've done something we don't know about."
"Let's not get involved."
"I don't want to lose my privileges."
"I heard they were threatening lawsuits."
"It's a private matter."
"They're not here anymore—why are we still talking about it?"

This is how institutions protect themselves:

Not by defending their decisions—but by **discouraging the questions.**

Harmony Over Honesty

Skidaway sells the idea that harmony is the highest virtue.

It's in the language of Club events.

It's in the messaging from leadership.

It's even in the bylaws.

But harmony without justice is **not peace**.

It's performance.

It's manufactured consensus, enforced through fear of exclusion.

And when harmony becomes the metric for governance, **truth becomes a threat.**

That's why Wilhelm's post had to disappear.

That's why Susanne's injury had to be forgotten.

That's why no one speaks publicly about what happened.

Because in this Club, asking "What's fair?" is seen as more dangerous than what's actually unfair.

The Real Cost of the Illusion

The Club has not just lost two members.

It has lost something greater: **its credibility**.

It has demonstrated that:

- Status does not protect you.
- Kindness does not shield you.
- Decades of good standing can be erased in 48 hours.
- Transparency is not a value—it's a liability.

And the lesson for every current and future member is simple:

You are safe—until you're not.

You belong—until you question.

You're celebrated—until your truth is inconvenient.

That's not a community.

That's a **transaction** with a smiling face.

A Mirror for Every Gated Community

The Haberkorn story is not unique to The Club.

It's happening in HOAs.
In private clubs.
In alumni boards.
In churches.
In golf resorts and social organizations across the country.

Institutions that present unity—but enforce obedience.

Places where image trumps ethics.
Where bylaws become weapons.
Where governance is a stage show for comfort, not justice.

This book is not just about what happened to two people.

It's a **mirror** held up to every reader who thinks, "That could never happen to me."

Because it can.

Because it did.

Because it's still happening.

In **Part III: Legality – The Labyrinth of the Legal System**, we leave The Club behind and enter the courtroom.

There, we discover that the system designed to protect rights is often too overwhelmed, too technical, or too indifferent to act.

We trace the lawsuits, the rulings, the denials—and how the same forces that silenced truth at The Club **are** *enshrined in law and precedent.*

Because The Club was just the beginning.

"They sold a brand of belonging—but delivered a culture of quiet exile."

— Prayer for Relief: ChatGPT

Part III: Legality

Chapter 1: First Steps

When the Doors of Justice Open with a Disclaimer

Wilhelm and Susanne Haberkorn never imagined they would spend their retirement years in court.

They didn't set out to sue anyone.

They weren't looking for a payday.

They didn't want a courtroom battle, a docket number, or a legal fight that would span years and generate over **16,000 pages** of filings.

All they wanted was an acknowledgment.

An apology.

A process.

But when those things were denied—and when silence was replaced by expulsion—there was only one place left to go: **the courts**.

And so, two long-standing members of a private coastal Club became **pro se litigants**—not because they wanted to represent themselves, but because **no one else would.**

The Myth of Accessible Justice

We're taught that the courts are open to all.

That justice is blind.

That everyone, regardless of wealth or title, has a right to be heard.

But once you step into the legal system without a lawyer, that illusion crumbles fast.

The language is foreign.
The rules are unforgiving.
The deadlines are absolute.

There are no greeters. No guides. No welcome packet for "first-time plaintiffs."

Just a clerk's window, a list of procedural requirements, and the cold certainty that **if you get even one step wrong—you will not be heard.**

The Early Missteps

Wilhelm's first filings were clear, heartfelt, and legally sound in their **substance**.

But the system cares just as much about **format**.

A missing certificate of service.

An improperly labeled motion.

A document submitted by mail instead of e-filed.

These errors—small, technical, understandable—became landmines.

Judges didn't address the injury.

They didn't review the forum post.

They didn't examine the timeline of the expulsion.

Instead, they dismissed claims because a response was filed one day late. Because an amended complaint "did not relate back." Because jurisdiction was disputed by The Club and accepted without scrutiny.

And so, **the truth was never reached**.

Because the road there was blocked with red tape.

Becoming the Lawyer You Can't Afford

Hiring an attorney seemed, at first, like the obvious next step.

But private Club cases are complicated. They involve bylaw interpretation, nonprofit law, discovery disputes, and defamation defenses—all niche and time-consuming.

Many lawyers had a conflict of interest; they were either Club members or frequent guests of members at The Club.

Others said, "This is a political hot potato. We'll pass."

So Wilhelm made the only choice he had left: **he studied the law himself**.

He learned to draft motions, respond to oppositions, and file appendices.

Not because he wanted to be a lawyer.

Because he refused to be silenced.

And in doing so, he became what few courts know how to handle: a **pro se litigant who wouldn't go away**.

The Double Standard

Judges often view self-represented plaintiffs with skepticism. They assume emotion overrules logic. They expect sloppiness, tantrums, and conspiracy theories.

So when Wilhelm filed documents meticulously citing law, precedent, and process, it didn't earn him respect.

It earned him suspicion.

When he filed multiple briefs defending himself against baseless accusations, the court called it "overfilling."

When he asked for the rules to be followed, he was called "litigious."

And yet, when The Club failed to produce discovery?

When their witnesses contradicted themselves?

When their process violated multiple state statutes?

The court shrugged.

Because institutions are given the benefit of the doubt.

Individuals are not.

The Toll of Going It Alone

Pro se litigation is exhausting.

It's reading case law at midnight.

It's weekends lost to formatting exhibits.

It's facing a wall of lawyers at hearings—each billing $400 an hour—while you stand alone with a binder.

It's knowing that one typo could undo a year of work.

It's feeling not just outnumbered—but **unwelcome** in the very space where justice is supposed to live.

And for Susanne—dealing with cognitive decline, physical injury, and emotional devastation—the toll was incalculable.

This was not justice.

It was **attrition by design**.

Why They Kept Going

So why continue?

Why not walk away?

Because walking away meant validating the lie.

It meant allowing an injury to go unaddressed.

It meant letting an expulsion stand that was built on distortion, silence, and cowardice.

It meant saying: *Yes, we accept that institutions can do this to people—and get away with it.*

And Wilhelm refused.

He didn't need to win a verdict to make his point.

He just needed the system to **see them**.

To recognize that:

- The accident happened.
- The process was broken.
- The governance failed.
- The silence harmed.

Even if the court didn't rule in their favor, the record would show the truth.

Because The Club had erased them, but the docket would not.

From Naïveté to Warrior

At the start, Wilhelm believed that facts would prevail.

That reasonable people—given the full story—would choose fairness.

He believed in systems. In process. In the idea that courts were a safeguard when private power failed.

But the deeper he went, the more he saw the truth:

Justice requires more than evidence. It requires persistence. And sometimes, a willingness to stand alone.

He became fluent in law not to win, but to survive.

He became strategic not to fight—but to **be allowed to speak.**

He entered the courthouse naive.

He walked out a warrior.

In the next chapter, **"The Legal Maze,"** we'll map the full terrain: how well-resourced institutions weaponize motion practice, delay tactics, and technical dismissals to avoid being held accountable.

Because truth may be your compass.

But in the legal labyrinth, the path to justice is anything but straight.

"In the legal arena, ignorance is punished. Learning is survival."

— Prayer for Relief: ChatGPT

Chapter 2: The Legal Maze

When the System Doesn't Care Why You're Here, Only How You Got In

If the legal system were a house, justice would be locked in the attic—and the stairs would be made of paper.

Wilhelm and Susanne Haberkorn entered that house believing they'd be heard; the facts would speak for themselves. That the courts would help them peel away the distortions of The Club and expose the truth underneath.

But they soon learned that **facts don't matter if the paperwork isn't perfect.**

And the system doesn't want your story.

It wants **your format, your form, your filing date—and your patience when none of it works in your favor**.

A Forest of Paper, Not Principles

Once the first complaint was filed, the flood began.

- Motions to dismiss.
- Motions to strike.
- Motions for protective orders.
- Discovery objections.
- Responses to motions.
- Replies to responses.

Each document, a new branch in a legal forest that seemed to grow overnight.

Each response from The Club was meticulously designed to do one thing: **avoid the facts.**

They didn't argue Susanne hadn't fallen.

They didn't argue Wilhelm's post was threatening.

They argued:

- That the original complaint didn't cover the right claims.
- That new claims didn't "relate back" under Georgia law.
- That deadlines were missed—even by days.
- That jurisdiction was lacking.

Their goal wasn't to prove innocence.

It was to **win by attrition**.

And in the legal system, that strategy works—especially against pro se litigants.

The Explosion of Technicality

In a world of moral clarity, the Haberkorns' story is simple:

- A member was injured.
- The Club failed to respond.
- Her spouse posted about it.
- The Club retaliated.

But the court's world is different.

There, a case can be dismissed not because it's untrue—but because it wasn't **properly pled**.

- Filed one day late? Denied.
- Used the wrong caption? Rejected.
- Failed to request a particular kind of relief in the right paragraph? Too bad.

Each procedural landmine is invisible—until you step on it.

And once you do, **the merits vanish beneath the rubble.**

The Weaponization of Delay

The Club's attorneys used a classic institutional playbook:

- Ask for extensions.
- Delay discovery.
- Argue jurisdiction.
- Demand specificity.
- File counter-motions.
- Create confusion.

Every motion became a smokescreen.

Every delay was designed to exhaust Wilhelm's time, energy, and resources.

They didn't need to answer the hard questions.

They just needed to **run out the clock**.

And the court—overwhelmed, understaffed, and steeped in tradition—played along.

The Statute of Limitations Trap

Perhaps the cruelest twist came with **O.C.G.A. § 14-3-621(4)**, the Georgia law governing membership expulsions from nonprofit organizations.

It requires any challenge to an expulsion to be filed within **one year** of the effective date.

The Club expelled Wilhelm and Susanne on **July 29, 2022**.

But Wilhelm didn't fully realize how procedurally flawed the expulsion was until months later—after the discovery stonewalling, after the forum post was mischaracterized, after the internal silence confirmed that no real process had ever taken place.

By the time the amended complaints were filed—including claims of due process violations and breach of contract—the one-year clock had ticked away.

Never mind that:

- The facts were clear.
- The injury was real.
- The expulsion was retaliatory.

The court refused to hear it.

Because the **calendar said no**.

Legal Loopholes as a Defense Strategy

The Club never had to say, "We did the right thing."

They only had to say, "You're too late to prove we didn't."

That's the difference between morality and legality.

In morality, the goal is to make things right.

In legality, the goal is to find **a rule to make things disappear**.

The Club succeeded—not because it was innocent—but because **it was better at playing the system**.

And the system—by design—rewards those who play it well.

The Emotional Weight of Legal Gaslighting

Over and over, Wilhelm read legal filings that described him as "hostile," "disruptive," "harassing."

All while the actual evidence—emails, the forum post, the timeline—told a completely different story.

But the court never reviewed the post.

Never heard his testimony.

Never examined Susanne's injury.

Because the avalanche of paper buried the substance.

And the only thing that mattered was whether the right documents were filed at the right time, with the right font, under the right rule.

The Invisibility of the Injured

Susanne's hip fracture? Irrelevant.

Her expulsion without notice? Procedurally unaddressed.

The timeline of silence? Not legally dispositive.

The forum post? Deleted, dismissed, and never reviewed in context.

The court system—built to interpret facts through law—**never reached the facts**.

Because institutions like The Club don't fight the truth directly.

They **out-procedure it**.

They don't have to say you're wrong.

They just have to say you didn't ask the question the right way, fast enough.

Justice as a Byproduct

The legal system isn't designed to dispense justice as its first priority.

It is designed to **process disputes through rules**.

If justice emerges from that process, it is often **accidental**.

That was the reality the Haberkorns learned—not in theory, but in filing after filing, ruling after ruling.

They brought the truth to court.

The court said, "You're out of time."

They brought injury.

The court said, “Irrelevant.”

They brought silence, facts, and erasure.

The court said, “Not our concern.”

Still, They Persisted

Despite the setbacks, Wilhelm kept filing—not to win by verdict, but to make the truth **a matter of public record**.

Because while The Club erased them from its internal systems, **the docket does not forget**.

Every filing is searchable.

Every exhibit is preserved.

Every misstep by The Club—every procedural dodge—now lives in ink and database.

That’s not vindication.

But it’s **resistance**.

It’s the refusal to let injustice go quietly.

In the previous chapter, we saw how a single forum post and a swift two-page expulsion letter shattered a 24-year relationship with a community—without hearing, without investigation, and without a single fact ever rebutted.

But that was only the beginning.

In the next chapter, **"Paper Explosion,"** we follow the trail of what happened next.
From one factual post grew a mountain of legal filings—motions, responses, orders, objections, and procedural maneuvers—**comprising 16,545 pages and 1,296 entries**.

Yet amid this avalanche of paper, one thing remained conspicuously absent: a direct response to the truth.

This is the story of a system that multiplies itself to avoid itself—and what it costs when justice is buried beneath bureaucracy.

"The law wasn't designed to be this complex. It was allowed to become this cruel."

— Prayer for Relief: ChatGPT

Chapter 3: Paper Explosion

It began with a fall.

And then, a forum post.

A factual, 1-page message posted by Wilhelm Haberkorn on the internal communications platform of The Club, describing the September 2021 accident that left his wife, Susanne, with a fractured hip. The post was not inflammatory. It contained no legal threats. No accusations. No demands. Just a public recounting of what had happened.

Then came a two-page expulsion letter—signed and sealed within 48 hours of that post being published and swiftly deleted.

And from there, the paper began to pile up.

What started as a simple injury, followed by a calm explanation and a reactionary punishment, grew into a judicial saga—spanning **multiple cases, two courts, and more than 16,545 pages of legal documents**, including **1,296 individual filings, motions, exhibits, affidavits, orders, and pleadings**.

But here's the most stunning part of it all:

Not a single page—**not one**—contains a substantive response by the defendants addressing the central facts:

- the accident,
- the absence of an investigation,
- the forum post's content,
- the legality of the expulsion, or

- the rights of Susanne Haberkorn.

This is not about a defense strategy.

This is about a **systemic failure**.

A legal process so bound in paperwork and proceduralism that it can **multiply itself 8,000 times over** from a single act of expression—without ever confronting the truth that act expressed.

📑 From One to Thousands: The Scale of Legal Paper Multiplication

Let us be precise. The court record across The Club case, the Executive Director, and the Board Member defendants includes:

- **16,545 total pages** filed into the record
- **1,296 individually docketed records**
- Documents spanning nearly two years
- Motions to dismiss, responses, procedural defenses, court-issued orders, and repeated exchanges over **form**, not substance

To contextualize this visually:

- A single banker's box holds ~300 pages. This record equates to **over 55 boxes**.
- Laid end-to-end, these pages would stretch more than **1,400 feet**, longer than four football fields.
- They stem from an expulsion triggered by a **two-page letter**—itself prompted by a **one-page post**.

That’s not litigation.

That’s **legal bloat**—a system whose self-sustaining inertia replaces resolution with ritual.

🏛 What the Paper Doesn’t Do

You might assume that somewhere in those thousands of pages, the defense addressed the allegations.

They did not.

Nowhere in the record does The Club or its officers:

- Deny that Susanne fell on a poorly maintained court,
- Provide an accident report,
- Explain why no investigation was initiated,
- Justify the forum post's deletion,
- Address the procedural legality of Wilhelm’s expulsion without a hearing,
- Explain why Susanne—who was not named in the expulsion letter—was also removed,
- Rebut the forum post’s content with facts.

In short, the **defendants never contested the narrative**.

Instead, they contested:

- Jurisdiction,
- Standing,
- Filing deadlines,
- Notice technicalities,
- The right of Wilhelm to represent his wife in court,

- And other **meta-legal abstractions** that let process substitute for accountability.

What they submitted was not a defense.

It was a wall.

🕰 Time as the Hidden Cost

Consider what it takes to **respond** to that much paperwork.

For the court: thousands of pages to sift, docket, schedule, and partially read.

For the plaintiff: a nearly impossible task for a pro se litigant with no assistant, no paralegal, and no secretary—just ten fingers and the ticking clock of procedural deadlines.

For the system: hours of wasted judicial bandwidth on **paperwork management**, not justice.

And for justice itself: **delay**, **deflection**, and **denial** by accumulation.

The burden shifts not to the side with the best facts, but to the side with **less paper to carry**.

💸 Cost as a Barrier to Entry

Let's talk money.

Defending 16,545 pages of litigation—regardless of merit—requires **substantial institutional infrastructure**. Based on standard legal billing rates and document handling protocols, the estimated cost of producing and managing that paper volume ranges between **$560,000 and $935,000+** for the defendants.

That includes:

- Attorney labor (estimated at 1,300+ hours)
- Paralegal support (up to 300 hours)
- Document management systems
- Filing fees
- Strategic litigation meetings
- Time spent reviewing, revising, and reproducing documents

Now contrast that with the estimated cost for a **pro se litigant using AI tools** to generate the same document volume:

Category	Estimated Cost (AI-Assisted Pro Se)
ChatGPT Subscription (1 year)	$240
Home Printing/Digital Prep	$150 – $300
Filing Fees (multiple motions/cases)	$1,000 – $2,500
Optional Expert Review (as needed)	$500 – $1,000
Total Cost Range	**$1,890 – $4,040**

This means the **plaintiff litigated at less than 1%** of the cost incurred by the defense—and still managed to **outfile,**

outlast, and out-argue their institutional counterparts on several procedural fronts.

This is not a story of frivolous litigation.

It is a story of what happens when a citizen armed with truth and technology confronts a system addicted to volume.

⚖️ A Court That Never Ruled

Even with all this paper, the courts never ruled on:

- Whether the expulsion was lawful,
- Whether the forum post constituted a "legal threat,"
- Whether due process was afforded,
- Whether intra-corporate privilege was misused to block claims,
- Whether the injuries and damages were preventable or acknowledged.

Instead, the only ruling of finality—the one closing the "Club Case"—was based on a procedural bar: the **statute of limitations** had run.

That was it.

The rest remain open, unresolved, or procedurally dismissed.

Justice was not done.

It was simply timed out.

🖇️ What the Paper Explosion Really Reveals

This chapter does not claim that the defense orchestrated a deliberate flood of filings to overwhelm the plaintiff. That would be speculative.

But it **does** assert that the system permitted—perhaps even encouraged—a form of litigation in which:

- **Volume displaces truth,**
- **Procedure displaces facts,**
- And **survival depends not on who is right, but who can afford to keep filing.**

This is not unique to this case.

It is endemic to a legal system that measures fairness in pages, not principles.

🧭 Conclusion: The Forum Post Was Heard—But Not Read

The greatest irony of all is that the **two original documents—the forum post and the expulsion letter—still say everything**.

In just three pages, they capture the central injustice.
In over 16,000 that followed, no one contradicted them.

So why did the paper explode?

Because the system doesn't know how to function without it.
Because complexity has become its own justification.
Because in the absence of a courtroom designed to hear the truth, it will settle for reading **everything but the truth**.

This chapter is a record of that reckoning.

A reminder that sometimes, fewer words **say more**.

And a warning: if the system can break down one factual post into 16,545 pieces of paper without addressing a single allegation, it's not just inefficient.

It's broken.

In the next chapter, **"Silenced by Privilege," we'll** explore the most insidious shield institutions use to silence dissent: the claim that internal communication and decision-making are immune from scrutiny.

Because when organizations can hide behind "private deliberation," **the truth becomes off-limits by design**.

"When systems rely on volume to win, truth doesn't stand a chance."

— Prayer for Relief: ChatGPT

Chapter 4:Silenced by Privilege

When the Truth Is Locked in a Room You Can't Enter

Imagine a world where you are accused of misconduct, removed from your community, and defamed on paper—and then told that **you can't know who said what, or why**.

That world is real.

It's made possible by a legal doctrine called **intra-corporate privilege**.

Originally designed to protect confidential conversations among corporate decision-makers, intra-corporate privilege now functions as a **shield against accountability** in nonprofits, clubs, HOAs, churches, and private boards.

And in the case of Wilhelm and Susanne Haberkorn, it was the very mechanism that allowed The Club to **silence justice without ever proving innocence**.

What Is Intra-Corporate Privilege?

At its core, intra-corporate privilege protects internal communications within a corporation—such as emails, meeting notes, or deliberations—when those communications are part of the organization's decision-making process.

The idea is simple: leaders must be able to discuss matters candidly without fear of discovery.

But like many legal doctrines, it's been **warped by convenience**.

In practice, this privilege has become **a legal black box**, where accountability goes to die.

You can be expelled from a club.
Defamed in writing.
Accused of vague "hostility."

And yet, when you request to know:

- Who made the allegations?
- What evidence was reviewed?
- What was said about you?

The answer is: *"That's privileged."*

The Wall Wilhelm Hit

In discovery, Wilhelm asked for basic information:

- The names of the individuals who discussed his expulsion.
- Notes from the Member Standards Committee.
- Emails between Executive Director and the Board.
- Any draft language of the expulsion letter.
- Records showing why Susanne's membership was revoked.

The Club's answer?

Intra-corporate privilege.

They claimed that all such communications were internal governance discussions—and therefore exempt from discovery.

This meant that Wilhelm couldn't confront his accusers.
Couldn't challenge their reasoning.
Couldn't see the documentation used to justify expelling him.

In other words, **he could be judged—but never shown the evidence.**

The Original Purpose, Lost in Practice

Intra-corporate privilege was never meant to enable injustice.

It was created to protect strategy—not secrecy.

To guard sensitive business planning—not cover up procedural failure.

But in governance spaces where there is no external oversight—such as private clubs—the privilege is now routinely used to **hide wrongdoing, suppress dissent, and dodge legal exposure.**

It has become:

- A reason not to disclose emails.
- A justification for withholding minutes.
- A catch-all shield for "anything inconvenient."

And judges, overwhelmed and overworked, often accept it at face value—without asking whether the privilege is being abused.

When Transparency Becomes a Threat

The Club couldn't deny Susanne fell.
It couldn't deny Wilhelm's forum post existed.

But it could refuse to answer questions about:

- What its leadership said privately.
- Whether retaliation was discussed.
- Whether the Board had concerns about liability.
- Whether the decision to expel was rushed, coerced, or even unanimous.

In short, it could block every path to the **truth behind the truth**.

Because when decisions are hidden behind the veil of privilege, truth becomes **a protected asset of the powerful**.

How This Plays Out in Court

When Wilhelm tried to compel The Club to produce internal emails and Board communications, The Club argued:

"These materials are part of The Club's internal governance process. Disclosing them would chill candid discussion."

It didn't matter that:

- He was the subject of the discussion.
- The content affected his rights.
- The outcome had real reputational and legal consequences.

The Club didn't need to prove the communications were justified—just that they existed **inside the bubble**.

And the court agreed.

Which meant The Club never had to explain:

- Why was the decision made in 48 hours?
- Who influenced it?
- What process, if any, was followed?
- Whether they knew they were violating Georgia law.

The result? **A procedurally perfect injustice.**

When Privilege Replaces Process

Here's the deeper danger.

Intra-corporate privilege gives organizations an incentive to:

- Move discussions off the record.
- Keep no minutes.
- Funnel decisions through narrow channels.
- Avoid written process entirely.

Because **no record means no liability.**

It encourages silence—not fairness.

Obfuscation—not governance.

And when that becomes standard, the organization ceases to serve its members. It serves only **its brand and its leadership's self-preservation**.

A Legal Loophole With Human Cost

For the Haberkorns, intra-corporate privilege meant:

- Their expulsion would never be explained.
- The people responsible would never face scrutiny.
- The false accusations would never be challenged.

Because The Club didn't have to defend the decision.

It only had to **hide the conversation** that led to it.

That is not justice.

It is **a loophole dressed in legal robes.**

And until courts begin to interrogate how intra-corporate privilege is applied in nonprofits and social organizations, this injustice will continue—quietly, legally, relentlessly.

What Needs to Change

The solution isn't to abolish intra-corporate privilege.

It's to **limit its scope**:

- Apply it to strategy, not personnel decisions.
- Require a threshold of transparency in expulsion or discipline cases.
- Mandate disclosure when membership rights are affected.
- Give courts tools to review documents *in camera* (privately) to prevent abuse.

Because when private organizations can act like governments—taxing, expelling, controlling access—**they must be held to a higher standard of process.**

And when that process is shielded by privilege, it's not just the member who suffers.

It's democracy by another name that gets betrayed.

In the next chapter, **"Shielded Nonprofits,"** we go deeper into the legal structure that protects organizations like The Club—even when they act unjustly.

Because in Georgia and across the country, nonprofits enjoy immunity, discretion, and legal leeway that make it nearly impossible to hold them accountable—unless the law itself is reformed.

"When a corporation speaks with one voice, it can silence many."

— Prayer for Relief: ChatGPT

Chapter 5: Shielded Nonprofits

When the Law Becomes the Problem

There's a strange irony buried in the Haberkorn case.

The law that should have protected them—the law that governs nonprofit organizations in Georgia—**was the very thing that protected The Club instead**.

Not because The Club acted rightly.

Not because the facts weren't on the Haberkorns' side.

But because the law, by design, grants nonprofits **extraordinary discretion and immunity**—even when they violate their own rules, or ignore basic principles of fairness.

This chapter explores how these laws work, how they were weaponized in this case, and why reform is not only overdue—it's urgent.

The Illusion of Accountability

Nonprofits like The Club are governed under **The Georgia Nonprofit Corporation Code**, particularly **O.C.G.A. Title 14, Chapter 3**.

On the surface, this statute seems balanced. It requires that:

- Members have rights.
- Due process is respected.
- Expulsions must include notice and an opportunity to be heard (**§ 14-3-621**).

But here's the catch:

While the law outlines those requirements, it **does not provide teeth**.

If an organization ignores them?

If it fails to notify members?

If it doesn't hold a hearing?

The law **doesn't mandate consequences**—unless the injured party can prove, within a year and with procedural perfection, that the organization's actions violated a narrowly interpreted standard.

And the courts? More often than not, **defer to the nonprofit**.

That deference is the flaw in the system.

Deference Over Evidence

In Wilhelm's litigation, The Club never proved it had followed a fair process.

It couldn't produce minutes, votes, or documentation of member standards being applied objectively.

And yet, the court dismissed claims—not because The Club proved its case, but because **the law doesn't require it to**.

It simply had to say:

"We made this decision internally."

And unless Wilhelm could **disprove their internal reasoning with admissible evidence**, he had no claim.

But how can you disprove something **you're not allowed to see?**

That's the double-bind built into nonprofit law:

- Internal decisions are private.
- External challenges require internal evidence.
- But internal evidence is protected.

It's not just unfair—it's **structurally rigged**.

The Bylaws Aren't a Contract (Until They Are)

Many members of private clubs believe their bylaws are like a contract: binding, enforceable, and reciprocal.

But courts often treat bylaws more like **guidelines**—unless the organization itself wants to enforce them.

When Wilhelm cited multiple bylaw violations—lack of notice, lack of hearing, lack of Board transparency—The Club claimed:

"We followed our process."

And when challenged?

They said:

"Even if we didn't, bylaws are internal matters."

But in defending the expulsion, they quoted those same bylaws to justify removing him.

So which is it?

Are bylaws enforceable, or not?

In practice, the law lets nonprofits have it both ways:

- Enforce rules against members.
- Ignore rules when challenged.

That's not a governance structure.

It's a **trap**.

The Statutory Minefield

The key statute in this case was **O.C.G.A. § 14-3-621**, which governs disciplinary actions against nonprofit members.

It requires:

- Reasonable process.
- Notice of the alleged infraction.
- An opportunity for the member to respond.
- And a one-year statute of limitations for any legal challenge.

But there are no enforcement mechanisms.

No requirement for recordkeeping.

No penalty for skipping steps.

And courts are reluctant to impose standards unless **gross misconduct** can be proven—which is nearly impossible without internal access.

So even when a member is expelled:

- Without notice.
- Without evidence.
- In retaliation for protected speech.

The court may still say:
"Sorry. The Club acted within its discretion."

Immunity in the Name of Service

The original intent behind nonprofit protections was noble.

These laws were created to:

- Encourage volunteer governance.
- Reduce frivolous lawsuits.
- Protect boards from undue liability.

But today, these protections are often **used to shield negligence, arrogance, and silence**.

Boards aren't held to ethical standards.

They're held to **the appearance of discretion**.

And when discretion is abused?
There's no recourse—unless the harmed party can navigate complex filings, hit precise deadlines, and overcome a judicial culture that almost always says:

"We don't second-guess nonprofits."

A Private Court, with No Appeals

Think about it.

Wilhelm and Susanne were:

- Accused.
- Judged.
- Expelled.

By a **private entity**, with no independent oversight, and no external appeal.

They had no access to records.

No chance to respond.

No opportunity to speak before their name was erased from the roster.

And the state of Georgia said:
"That's legal."

Because legally, nonprofits are allowed to govern themselves.

But ethically?

Morally?

Humanely?

That's a different conversation.

One the law has not yet caught up with.

The Cost of Legal Deference

By deferring to nonprofits:

- The courts allow injustice.
- The law emboldens secrecy.
- Institutions are trained to fear liability more than they fear harming members.

The Haberkorns didn't lose in court because they were wrong.

They lost because **the court said it wasn't its job to interfere.**

That's not neutrality.

It's **abdication**.

And it tells every nonprofit in the state:

- You can expel members without hearing them.
- You can erase records of wrongdoing.
- You can weaponize bylaws selectively.

Just don't leave a paper trail.

And make sure you call it "internal governance."

A Call for Legislative Reform

It doesn't have to be this way.

Legislatures could:

- Require documentation of disciplinary action.
- Limit blanket deference to internal decisions.
- Create minimum standards for transparency.
- Extend the statute of limitations when discovery is delayed by the nonprofit's own silence.

- Allow judicial review of expulsions when basic procedural fairness is questioned.

Because justice should not end at the gates of a private community.

And nonprofits should not be allowed to silence their members **under color of law**.

In the next chapter, **"Court Indifference,"** we examine the final barrier: a judicial system that treats pro se litigants like nuisances and institutions like citizens of higher standing.

The Haberkorns brought truth. The Club brought lawyers.

And the court? It brought a stamp that said "Dismissed."

> *"They hid behind statutes designed to help them help others. Instead, they helped themselves."*
>
> — Prayer for Relief: ChatGPT

Chapter 6: Court Indifference

When Justice Is a Game, and You Don't Know the Rules

The Haberkorns brought a simple request to court: **Let us be heard.**

They didn't ask for special treatment.
They didn't expect sympathy.
They expected only what the law promises to all: **a fair shot.**

What they received instead was a system that looked at them—not as citizens seeking justice—but as **a procedural inconvenience.**

They weren't just outnumbered.

They were **out-respected**.

The Disadvantage of Being Right

There's a myth that the legal system protects truth.

That if you are right, the law will eventually bend toward your favor.

But Wilhelm quickly learned that being right means nothing if:

- Your brief is formatted incorrectly.
- You cite the wrong subsection.
- You miss a filing deadline.
- You don't know when or how to object.

Being correct is **not enough**.

And when you don't wear a suit, carry a bar card, or speak in the language of the court, your truth often gets treated like **noise**.

Even when it's clearer, stronger, and better supported than the opposition.

The Tone Tax

Courts expect pro se litigants to be:

- Precise.
- Polite.
- Respectful.
- Submissive.

They also expect them to absorb condescension, procedural rebukes, and even judicial irritation—**without showing emotion**.

Because the moment a self-represented person pushes back too hard, raises their voice, or shows frustration, they risk being labeled:

"Hostile."
"Disruptive."
"Unprofessional."

And so Wilhelm—wrongfully expelled, misrepresented in writing, and denied discovery—had to argue as if **none of it affected him personally**.

As if his wife's injury, the lies, the deletions, and the silence were just "legal matters," not **the ruin of everything they had built**.

That's the double standard:

Lawyers can be aggressive.

Institutions can be dismissive.

But a pro se litigant must **remain perfect in demeanor—even while being ignored**.

The Bench Is Not Always Neutral

Many judges begin with an implicit bias:
If you don't have an attorney, your case probably isn't serious.

And that bias shapes everything:

- How closely your filings are read.
- How much leeway you get on formatting.
- Whether your arguments are considered generous interpretations—or frivolous stretches.

Wilhelm found himself being corrected, not heard.

Judges waved away complex timelines with:

"This should have been in your original complaint."

Or dismissed valid procedural violations with:

"That's an internal Club matter."

It wasn't that the judges were malicious.

It's that the system is built for efficiency—not fairness.

And pro se litigants, by default, are seen as **speed bumps in the calendar**.

The Disproportionate Deference

When The Club's lawyers filed responses, courts accepted them as structured, reasoned, professional.

When Wilhelm filed replies citing law, quoting The Club's own bylaws, and pointing out contradictions?

The court asked:

"Why wasn't this raised sooner?"

Or worse:

"This seems argumentative."

Deference flowed in one direction—toward the institution with resources.

Not toward the citizen fighting for their rights alone.

That's not neutrality.

That's **systemic favoritism** disguised as "judicial discretion."

The Quiet Practice of Judicial Dismissal

The most common outcome for pro se cases?

Dismissal without hearing the facts.

Not because the facts are weak.

But because the pleadings don't match expectations.

- You cite the wrong rule? Dismissed.
- You refile with corrections? Dismissed again—too late.
- You amend to include claims that arise from the same timeline? Denied—"doesn't relate back."

In the Haberkorn case, this pattern played out again and again.

- Judges ruled on **procedure**, never substance.
- No one examined the forum post in its full context.
- No court considered whether **Susanne's expulsion was legal**.
- No discovery ruling ever compelled The Club to turn over internal communications.

The courts didn't say The Club acted appropriately.

They just said Wilhelm hadn't jumped through **enough hoops in the right order**.

That isn't a legal system.

It's a **labyrinth with a trapdoor at the start.**

The Reality of "Access to Justice"

Access to justice means more than the ability to file.

It means the ability to:

- Be taken seriously.
- Have your arguments heard.
- Be judged by substance, not style.
- Face equal scrutiny as your opposition.

But for pro se litigants, that access is theoretical.

Because unless you can:

- Decode the local rules,
- Predict the courtroom culture,
- Anticipate opposing tactics,
- And meet legal expectations written by and for lawyers…

You won't reach justice.

You'll reach **a dismissal order with your name misspelled.**

Still, He Showed Up

Despite the system's indifference…

Despite the procedural tricks…

Despite the biased tone of some rulings…

Wilhelm kept showing up.

To protect his wife's story.

To prove that what happened to them was not a fluke—but a **predictable failure of power unchecked**.

He didn't ask to be a legal warrior.

He became one because **no one else would fight for them**.

And though the court never gave him the justice they deserved…

He left behind something powerful:

A **record**.

An **indictment**—not of one Club, but of a legal culture that rewards complexity and punishes clarity.

What We Must Confront

The Haberkorn case reveals a painful truth:

You can be right.

You can be wronged.

You can follow the law, quote the law, defend the law—

And still, the court can tell you:

"That's not our problem."

Because you didn't format it right.

Because you didn't ask fast enough.

Because you didn't hire someone who charges $400 an hour.

That's not a justice system.

That's **a system that hopes the self-represented just go away.**

In the next chapter, **"Silencing Tactics,"** we reveal how courts and institutions don't just ignore pro se litigants—they sometimes **punish them for continuing to speak**.

Because when silence fails, the system has one more tool:

Retribution.

"Pro se doesn't mean powerless. But too often, it means ignored."

— Prayer for Relief: ChatGPT

Chapter 7: Silencing Tactics

When Persistence Becomes a Punishable Offense

In a just world, persistence is a virtue.

But in the legal system—especially when you're representing yourself—**persistence is often treated as provocation**.

If you file too much, you're called disruptive.
If you challenge procedural mistakes, you're labeled argumentative.
If you point out contradictions, you're accused of wasting judicial resources.

For Wilhelm Haberkorn, standing up for his wife, defending their rights, and pressing for answers wasn't just dismissed—it was punished.

Because in the world of pro se litigation, the most powerful tool the courts have to silence you is not a ruling.

It's a **sanction**.

What Is a Sanction?

Sanctions are meant to penalize litigants who abuse the court process—those who file in bad faith, who lie, who use the court to harass or obstruct.

But in practice, sanctions have become a way to **discipline dissent**.

To discourage repeat filings.

To shut down unrepresented litigants who refuse to “stay in their lane.”

To **send a message**: Stop.

And if you don’t?

The consequences can be devastating:

- Fines.
- Orders barring further filings.
- Public reprimands.
- Permanent dismissal with prejudice.
- A chilling effect on others' thinking about fighting back.

The Paper Cuts That Became a Whip

Wilhelm was meticulous.

He cited law. He submitted evidence. He followed court rules to the best of his ability.

But because he was pro se—and because he *didn’t stop*—his filings were reframed.

From advocacy…
To “frivolous.”
From diligence…
To “vexatious.”
From strategy…
To “harassment.”

The more he filed, the less the court listened.

Not because his filings lacked merit—but because they challenged a system **not used to being challenged by someone without a legal degree.**

And eventually, the court did what institutions do when they tire of dissent:

It sanctioned him.

The Message Behind the Sanction

The purpose of the sanction wasn't to correct behavior.

Wilhelm hadn't lied. He hadn't disobeyed orders. He hadn't abused process.

He had only done what the system allegedly welcomes: **used his voice**.

But the court wasn't interested in hearing from him anymore.

So the sanction became **the closing gavel.**

A way of saying:

"We've heard enough."

Even if **nothing had actually been heard at all.**

Silence by Intimidation

Sanctions aren't just punishments.

They're deterrents.

And not just to the litigant.

To **everyone else watching.**

They signal:

- "Don't file like this person."
- "Don't question outcomes."
- "Don't represent yourself unless you're prepared to lose more than your case."

It creates a culture where:

- Institutions are protected.
- Judges go unchallenged.
- Errors are buried beneath fear.

And when people like Wilhelm are sanctioned **for insisting on process**, it tells the public:

"The courtroom is not for you."

Unless you can pay.

Unless you can behave.

Unless you can **stay quiet when told.**

Who Really Gets Protected?

Sanctions are justified when used against abuse.

But here, the abuse wasn't coming from Wilhelm.

It was coming from:

- A Club that erased an injured member.
- A Board that violated its own rules.
- A leadership team that deleted evidence and offered no explanation.
- A legal team that delayed, denied, and deflected every request for truth.

Yet none of these parties were sanctioned.

None were fined for refusing discovery.

None were punished for deleting records.

None were held accountable for weaponizing delay.

Only Wilhelm.

Because he **refused to go away quietly.**

Because he kept asking, "Where is the justice?"

The Cost of Retaliatory Sanctions

Sanctioning pro se litigants doesn't just silence them.

It breaks something deeper:

- It discourages civic engagement.
- It deters people from seeking redress.
- It trains citizens to believe that the law is not theirs.

And it sends a signal to institutions:
"Keep doing what you're doing—we won't interfere."

This doesn't protect the courts.

It undermines them.

It turns them from halls of justice into fortresses of exclusion.

Where only the privileged speak, and the persistent are punished.

What Wilhelm Showed Us

Despite being sanctioned, Wilhelm continued to advocate.

Not because he was trying to win in court—but because he was fighting **for the record**.

For truth.

For the next person who might walk this path.

He made his filings part of the permanent public story.
He forced The Club to respond.
He created a paper trail that could no longer be deleted, redacted, or ignored.

And even when the court pushed him away, the facts remained.

Because while sanctions can silence a voice…

They cannot silence **what actually happened.**

The Final Irony

The same system that refused to examine the evidence…

That ignored the procedural failures of The Club…

That rejected the pleas of an injured woman and her husband…

Had the gall to say, in effect:

"You're the problem. Not the process."

And that is the core of this chapter:

Justice wasn't denied by accident.

It was denied **by design.**

And the penalty for not accepting that reality was **a sanction**.

In the next chapter, **"Justice as Byproduct,"** we pivot from tragedy to hope.

We examine what went wrong not just in the Haberkorn case, but in the legal system itself—and how new tools like ChatGPT can arm the next generation of pro se litigants with the precision, clarity, and resilience they need to push back, file smarter, and win.

"Sanctions are supposed to deter abuse—not silence the abused."

— Prayer for Relief: ChatGPT

Chapter 8: Justice as Byproduct

Why the System Delivers Justice by Accident—And What That Means for the Rest of Us

We are raised to believe that justice is the end goal of the legal system.

That judges are impartial.
That laws are fair.
That courts are temples of reason where truth emerges through process.

But for Wilhelm and Susanne Haberkorn, the lesson was stark:

Justice is not the goal.

It is, at best, **a byproduct**—a fortunate accident that occurs only when:

- Procedures align perfectly,
- Timing is exact,
- Lawyers are skilled,
- Judges are open-minded,
- And the institution being challenged doesn't bury the truth first.

Otherwise?

Justice doesn't happen.

Not because it's denied—but because **it was never the point to begin with.**

What the System Is Really Designed For

The legal system is not designed to uncover truth.

It is designed to **manage conflict**.

- It prioritizes **process over principle**.
- It rewards those who know how to navigate the maze.
- It punishes mistakes, even innocent ones, with finality.

It is a machine built not to weigh right and wrong, but to enforce **rules of engagement**.

If you file the wrong form, your evidence doesn't matter.
If you miss a deadline, your injury becomes irrelevant.
If your argument lacks legal jargon, **your voice disappears**.

This is not an accident.

It is the system doing what it was built to do:
Filter, narrow, exclude, control.

And if justice emerges on the other side, it is **incidental**.

When the System Works Best—for Institutions

The institutions that thrive in this system:

- Have attorneys on retainer.
- Know how to delay.
- Use discovery as a weapon.
- Exploit statutes of limitation like a shield.
- Win cases not on merit, but on **maneuvering**.

The Club didn't "win" in court because it proved Wilhelm and Susanne were wrong.

It "won" because:

- They deleted the forum post before it could be reviewed.
- They never documented the expulsion process.
- They invoked privilege to hide internal communications.
- They ran out the one-year clock on O.C.G.A. § 14-3-621.
- They convinced the court to treat bylaws as private—even while using them to justify expulsion.

This wasn't victory through vindication.

It was **victory through architecture.**

A system rigged to **favor the comfortable**.

When the Facts Don't Matter

Let's be clear.

Susanne fell.

That's a fact.

The court was dangerous.
The Club ignored the injury.
Wilhelm posted a reasonable, factual message.
The post was deleted.
He was expelled without due process.
So was she.

These are not theories. They are truths.

But the court never examined those truths.

It dismissed claims on:

- Filing timelines.
- Jurisdictional interpretation.
- "Failure to state a claim."

At no point did a judge say:

"Let's look at the accident report."
"Let's evaluate the legitimacy of the expulsion process."
"Let's consider the harm done to a woman who never spoke, never violated a rule, and was still removed."

The merits of the case were irrelevant.

Because the process **never let them through the door.**

Justice as the Exception, Not the Rule

Most people assume courts deliver justice because we see stories where that happens.

But those stories are **rare**.

They make headlines because they're unusual.

Most outcomes aren't about justice.

They're about:

- Procedural closure.
- Risk management.

- Institutional preservation.

And for every person who gets a just ruling…

There are hundreds whose truths were perfectly valid, but whose filings weren't perfect enough.

The Haberkorns joined the ranks of the dismissed not because they didn't try hard enough—but because the system doesn't care how hard you try.

It cares **whether you play the game—and whether you do it with the right credentials**.

Justice for Sale

If Wilhelm had had $300,000 to spend on a top-tier attorney…

- His filings would've been polished.
- His motions would've hit every procedural mark.
- Discovery would've been compelled.
- The forum post would've been entered into the record immediately.
- Susanne's injury would've been evaluated within context.
- The Club's contradictions would've been cross-examined in court.

And maybe—just maybe—the result would've changed.

Not because the facts would be different.

But because **he would've had the right key to unlock the door.**

That is not justice.

That is **a market for outcomes**.

And it leaves everyone else standing outside, holding the truth like a useless ticket.

What We Learned

When Wilhelm and Susanne sought justice, they found:

- Silence.
- Delay.
- Obstruction.
- Redirection.
- Retaliation.
- Dismissal.
- Sanctions.

The system never examined the wrong.

It examined the paperwork.

And that told them everything they needed to know:

This system is not built to serve truth.

It's built to serve itself.

And justice, when it shows up, does so **despite the system—not because of it.**

What We Must Change

If we want justice to be the *goal*—not just the accident—we need:

- Procedural simplification for pro se litigants.
- Real enforcement of nonprofit transparency.
- Limits on intra-corporate privilege.
- Statutes of limitation that flex when discovery is delayed.
- Judges trained to engage substance before form.
- Court systems that *want* to hear from the public, not *punish* them for trying.

Until that happens, justice will remain an outlier.

Not the standard.

Not the goal.

Just the rare result of someone who **refused to give up**—even when every door was locked, and the people inside pretended they weren't home.

In **Part IV: Relief – A New Vision for Pro Se Power**, we reclaim the narrative.

Because while the courts may be indifferent and institutions may be protected, a new tool—AI—has emerged to arm the voiceless.

And when used well, it doesn't just level the playing field.

It rewrites the rules.

"The process has become the prize. And justice, the afterthought."

— Prayer for Relief: ChatGPT

Part IV: Relief

Chapter 1: Justice Reclaimed

Because the System Won't Change Unless We Change How We Fight It

By now, the story is painfully clear.

Susanne Haberkorn fell.
The Club turned away.
Wilhelm spoke up.
The Club retaliated.
The courts looked the other way.

This was not a story of bad luck.
It was a story of **structural failure**.

The system failed—not because it was broken, but because **it worked exactly as it was designed to.**

- Designed to protect institutions over individuals.
- Designed to reward legal fluency over lived truth.
- Designed to confuse, delay, and exhaust the self-represented.

It didn't matter that Wilhelm had the facts.
It didn't matter that Susanne had the injury.
It didn't matter that The Club had no evidence, no process, no justification.

They lost—not in truth, but in **procedure**.

And for most people, that's where the story ends.

But something happened on the other side of that failure—something powerful.

Wilhelm didn't just walk away.

He discovered a tool.

And through that tool, **he began to rewrite the odds**.

That tool was ChatGPT.

The Problem Wasn't the Law—It Was Access to It

The law wasn't invented to silence people like Wilhelm and Susanne.

It was meant to protect them.

But over time, the language of law became a **barrier instead of a bridge**.

Statutes turned into mazes.
Rules multiplied.
Deadlines tightened.
Formatting became sacred.
Substance got lost in style.

The average person couldn't understand the system, let alone use it.

Lawyers became translators.
Judges became gatekeepers.
And justice became **a luxury item**.

AI changes that.

Not because it changes the law.

But because it **changes who can use it.**

The Power of ChatGPT Isn't Magic—It's Leverage

When Wilhelm started using ChatGPT, he didn't find a genie.

He found a **partner**.

One that could:

- Explain statutes in plain language.
- Draft motions with correct formatting.
- Roleplay courtroom scenarios.
- Generate responses to opposing counsel.
- Highlight contradictions in filings.
- Create timelines from hundreds of documents.
- Spot procedural landmines before they detonate.

And it did all of that without billing him $400 an hour.

AI didn't remove the injustice.

But it gave Wilhelm the language of the system that had excluded him.

And once he had the language?

He could **speak back to power**.

AI Doesn't Make You a Lawyer—It Makes You Dangerous to the People Who Count on You Not Knowing

Institutions like The Club count on your ignorance.

They count on your inability to cite bylaws.
To understand nonprofit governance.
To respond to discovery objections.
To format a reply brief.

They count on you making mistakes—because mistakes **cost you your right to be heard.**

But when you use AI properly, you're no longer a nuisance.

You become **a litigant they can't afford to ignore**.

You know what motions to file.
You know what questions to ask.
You know when they're bluffing.

You don't need to be an expert.

You just need to stop being **invisible**.

The Courts Are Still Cold—But Now You Have Armor

Make no mistake: the courts are still skeptical of pro se litigants.

AI won't erase that bias.

But it will:

- Help you sound like you belong there.
- Help you file correctly the first time.
- Help you prepare for the questions a judge might ask.
- Help you answer those questions with precision, not panic.

It's not just about winning.

It's about **surviving the system long enough to tell your story.**

AI gives you that chance.

And for the first time, **you don't need permission to access power.**

Justice Won't Be Handed Down—It Has to Be Built Up

What Wilhelm learned, and what this book now offers, is simple:

Justice can't be expected from the system.

It must be **extracted from it.**

With the right prompts.
The right documents.
The right timelines.
The right persistence.

That's what ChatGPT made possible.

Not a shortcut.

A **strategy**.

Not a miracle.

A **method**.

And now that method can be shared with others who—like Wilhelm and Susanne—have been silenced, erased, or ignored.

What This Chapter Means for You

If you've ever:

- Been dismissed by a board.
- Been ignored by a court.
- Been retaliated against for speaking truth.
- Been labeled a problem for seeking answers.

This chapter is your turning point.

Because now you don't have to **ask** for power.

You can **build it yourself**.

And you can start **today**.

With:

- AI-generated legal prompts.
- Case-specific strategies.
- Drafts of motions.
- Discovery checklists.
- Advocacy tools.

All at your fingertips.

All with one free prompt:

"I'm representing myself. Help me fight back."

A New Chapter for Pro Se Justice

Wilhelm and Susanne didn't get their day in court.

But their case lit a fire.

It proved that institutions are vulnerable—not to lawsuits, but to **exposure**.

And AI gives everyday people the flashlight.

The court may not want to see you.

The board may want to pretend you don't exist.

But the page, the filing, the record?

It **can't ignore you** if you file it right.

And now, **you can.**

In the next chapter, **"Prompting for Power,"** we dive into the "how."

You'll learn how to write prompts that generate real results.
How to avoid generic answers.
How to turn a messy case file into a strategic plan.

Because you don't just need AI.

You need to know how to talk to it.

"Justice didn't fail because of a lack of truth. It failed because of a lack of tools."

— Prayer for Relief: ChatGPT

Chapter 2: Prompting for Power

Because the Right Prompt Can Open Doors That Were Slammed Shut

Imagine standing at the foot of a massive legal mountain—procedures winding like switchbacks, rules etched in stone, and no guide to lead you.

Now imagine a voice beside you that says:

"Tell me what happened. I'll help you take the first step."

That voice is ChatGPT.

Not a lawyer.
Not a miracle.
But a tool—a legal flashlight.
And if you know how to use it, it will light up pathways the legal system never showed you before.

This chapter teaches you how.

Because prompting isn't just about asking questions.
It's about **framing your truth in a way the system can understand.**

And in the legal world, **how you ask determines what you get.**

◆ The Anatomy of a Powerful Legal Prompt

A good legal prompt includes:

1. **Your Role** – "I am a pro se litigant…"
2. **Your Goal** – "Help me draft a motion to compel…"
3. **Your Context** – "The opposing party ignored discovery requests sent on [date]…"
4. **Your Tone** – "Make the language firm but respectful…"

When all four are present, ChatGPT can respond like a real assistant—not just a search engine.

Example – Weak Prompt:

"Write a legal motion."

Example – Strong Prompt:

"I am a pro se litigant in Georgia State Court. Help me draft a Motion to Compel Discovery under O.C.G.A. § 9-11-37. The defendant has failed to respond to discovery requests served on June 12. I want the motion to be respectfully worded but clearly show noncompliance."

Result: A properly structured draft that looks like it belongs in the courtroom.

◆ Use the Prompt Framework: FACTS – GOAL – TONE – FORMAT

Step	What to Include
Facts	Summarize the situation in 1–3 sentences.
Goal	Be specific: motion, summary, timeline, objection, etc.

Step	What to Include
Tone	Formal? Respectful? Assertive? Neutral? Say what tone you want.
Format	Memo? Timeline? Motion? Email to court? Letter to opposing counsel? Specify.

Prompt Template:

"I am a pro se litigant representing myself in [State] in [court type]. My case involves [brief description of dispute]. I need help drafting [goal]. Please make the tone [tone]. Return the response in [format]."

◆ ChatGPT Is a Mirror and a Mentor

Use AI not just to **generate**, but to **evaluate**.

Try This:

"Here is my draft Motion to Dismiss. Please review it for legal clarity, structure, and persuasive tone. Suggest edits that make it more effective in Georgia Superior Court."

ChatGPT will return suggestions based on real legal reasoning—even citing case law or Civil Practice Act rules if asked.

◆ Don't Stop at One Prompt—Refine

Think of prompting like cross-examination.

One question leads to another.

Start simple:

"What are the key elements of a wrongful expulsion claim under Georgia nonprofit law?"

Then go deeper:

"What specific cases in Georgia have addressed due process violations in club expulsions?"

Then apply:

"Based on those elements, do my facts support a claim?"

This is **legal analysis in motion**—and you're the one steering.

◆ Use ChatGPT to Simulate the Other Side

One of the most powerful uses of AI?
Role-playing your opposition.

"Pretend you are an attorney for The Club. Challenge my complaint. What procedural arguments would you raise? What would your motion to dismiss say?"

Then flip it:

"Now respond as me. Draft a reply defending the filing."

This back-and-forth builds resilience, anticipation, and clarity.

It's chess—not checkers.

◆ Prompt AI to Build Your Timeline

Courts love timelines.

They cut through noise and clarify patterns.

Feed ChatGPT your events:

- Sept 11, 2021 – Susanne falls on Court #19.
- Nov 8, 2021 – Executive Director informed via email.
- July 27, 2022 – Wilhelm posts on forum.
- July 29, 2022 – Expulsion letter issued.

Then say:

"Build this into a clean, chronological timeline suitable for filing or legal summary."

Result: A powerful exhibit that the judge can understand at a glance.

◆ Prompt AI to Decode Legalese

When you get a ruling or filing you don't understand:

"Explain this court order in plain English. What does it mean, and what do I need to do next?"

Or:

"Opposing counsel filed a demurrer. What is that, and how should I respond?"

AI becomes your in-the-moment legal interpreter—one who never sighs or condescends.

◆ Prompt AI to Draft Discovery Questions

Discovery is where cases are won.

Use prompts like:

"Create 10 interrogatories for a wrongful expulsion case involving a private Georgia club. Focus on process, bylaws, and member communications."

Then say:

"Now draft 10 requests for production of documents that reveal internal decision-making."

You're not guessing what to ask—you're generating **precision tools**.

◆ Prompt AI to Write Respectful but Firm Letters

Sometimes, you need to put the court or opposing counsel on notice.

"Draft a respectful letter to opposing counsel requesting overdue discovery responses. Include a warning that a motion to compel will be filed if no reply is received in 7 days."

Tone matters.

So say:

"Make it sound serious, not hostile."

ChatGPT becomes your **tone editor** as much as your legal writer.

◆ Use Prompts to Stay Organized

ChatGPT can help you manage overwhelm.

"Help me create a legal task list based on my filing deadlines and current motions. Include due dates and priorities."

Or:

"Generate a checklist of what I need before a hearing in Georgia State Court."

This is more than productivity—it's **mental peace.**

◆ Pro Tip: Ask ChatGPT to Pretend It's a Georgia Litigator

If you're in Georgia (or your state), use this framing:

"Act as a Georgia civil litigator experienced in nonprofit and expulsion law. Help me draft a complaint under O.C.G.A. § 14-3-621 based on the following facts…"

It adjusts its lens, tone, and detail level automatically.

Final Thought: Prompting Is Power

In court, what you say must be **accurate, strategic, and effective**.

ChatGPT helps you practice that—privately, instantly, and without fear.

Your story deserves to be told **legibly**.
Your claims deserve to be filed **correctly**.
Your arguments deserve to be **understood**.

Now you have the means.

Not a miracle.
Not a replacement for a lawyer.
But a **legal intelligence assistant**—ready 24/7.

And best of all?

It never treats you like you don't belong.

Because you do.

In the next chapter, **"Panic to Plan,"** we'll go from prompts to power-mapping. You'll learn how to structure your case like a litigator: with themes, timelines, legal elements, and fallback arguments—all built step-by-step with your new co-counsel.

"The law is a language. Prompts are how you learn to speak it."

— Prayer for Relief: ChatGPT

Chapter 3: Panic to Plan

When Clarity Becomes Your Strongest Weapon

Panic is what most people feel the moment they realize they'll have to represent themselves.

There's the fear of not knowing where to start.
The avalanche of paperwork.
The impossible deadlines.
The cold, technical language.
The realization that **your truth alone won't be enough**.

For Wilhelm and Susanne, that moment came after they were expelled from The Club. The truth was on their side—but the legal system didn't care unless it was presented **in the right way, at the right time, with the right structure.**

This chapter shows you how to build that structure—**with the help of AI.**

Because ChatGPT doesn't just answer legal questions.

It helps you turn confusion into clarity.
It helps you map out your case.
It helps you think like a strategist—not just a survivor.

🔹 What Is a Case Strategy?

A case strategy answers three questions:

1. **What am I trying to prove?**
2. **What are the legal elements of that claim?**

3. **What facts support those elements—and what documents prove them?**

This isn't about writing one motion.

It's about **building a narrative**—and matching it to **law and evidence.**

With ChatGPT, you don't need to guess.

You can prompt it to walk you through each step—and fill in the gaps along the way.

◆ Step 1: Identify Your Legal Claims

Ask:

"Based on this summary of events, what legal claims might apply under Georgia law?"

Then paste your facts.

ChatGPT will return potential causes of action:

- Breach of contract.
- Wrongful expulsion under O.C.G.A. § 14-3-621.
- Defamation.
- Negligence.
- Breach of fiduciary duty (by the board).

Then follow up with:

"What are the elements I must prove for each of these claims?"

Now you're working like a litigator—**mapping the law to your facts.**

◆ Step 2: Build Your Issue Tree

Ask ChatGPT to:

"Create a case strategy outline. For each claim, list the legal elements, the supporting facts from my case, and the evidence that could support each."

Example output:

Claim: Wrongful Expulsion

- **Element 1: Membership was terminated.**
  - Fact: Expulsion letter dated July 29, 2022.
  - Evidence: Club's own letter.
- **Element 2: Termination lacked required notice or hearing.**
  - Fact: No meeting, no opportunity to respond.
  - Evidence: Email records, absence of minutes.

Now you're not just telling your story.

You're **building your argument like a case file.**

◆ Step 3: Organize Your Facts into a Timeline

Ask:

"Organize the following facts into a timeline that highlights key legal milestones."

Paste your dates and events.

Ask ChatGPT to:

- Flag procedural failures.
- Align facts with claim elements.
- Create a chart you can use in motions, pleadings, or hearings.

Now you're **leading the court through your case.**

◆ Step 4: Identify What's Missing

Every good strategy includes a **gap check.**

Ask:

"Based on my claims and timeline, what factual or evidentiary gaps might weaken my case?"

ChatGPT might return:

- "You may need direct evidence that no hearing occurred."
- "Consider requesting minutes through discovery."
- "Testimony from other members may strengthen your claim of retaliation."

Now you're thinking proactively—**not reactively.**

You're plugging holes before the opposition points them out.

◆ Step 5: Prioritize Your Claims

If you file 12 causes of action, the court may lose focus—or patience.

Ask:

"Rank these legal claims by likelihood of success and strongest supporting evidence."

ChatGPT might say:

- "Wrongful expulsion is strongest, supported by clear documentation."
- "Negligence claim may be difficult due to lack of direct causation."
- "Breach of fiduciary duty may require board communication evidence."

This helps you decide what to **lead with**—and what to save for later.

◆ Step 6: Build Your Case Theory

A case theory is your story in one sentence.

Ask:

"Help me craft a one-sentence case theory summarizing my argument for a judge."

ChatGPT may return:

"The Club expelled me in retaliation for a factual, non-threatening forum post, without notice, hearing, or process, violating Georgia law and their own bylaws."

That's the core of every motion, every filing, every hearing.

You're not rambling.
You're **aiming.**

◆ Step 7: Anticipate Defenses

A strong case strategy includes your opposition's playbook.

Ask:

"What defenses might The Club raise against a wrongful expulsion claim? How can I prepare counterarguments?"

ChatGPT might list:

- Statute of limitations (O.C.G.A. § 14-3-621 – 1 year).
- "At-will" membership clause.
- Broad discretionary language in bylaws.
- Claim that post constituted legal threat.

Then you prompt:

"How do Georgia courts evaluate expulsion discretion under § 14-3-621?"

Now you're not just reacting.
You're **neutralizing threats before they're filed.**

◆ Step 8: Plan for Hearings or Mediation

Strategy isn't just for the page.

Ask:

"What should I bring to a pro se mediation for a wrongful expulsion case? What arguments resonate best with a neutral mediator?"

Or:

"How can I prepare an opening statement for a hearing that tells my story and hits the legal points?"

Let ChatGPT help you rehearse:

"Act as a skeptical judge. Challenge my claim and help me defend it."

Now you're building **courtroom confidence**, not just courtroom content.

◆ Step 9: Keep a Living Case Map

Ask ChatGPT to help you create and update a case map:

"Track my claims, facts, deadlines, documents filed, and pending motions in a single view."

This is your battlefield map.

You know what's filed.
You know what's due.
You know what's next.

And you're never surprised again.

◆ From Chaos to Control

The court system can make you feel small.

It's designed to.

But when you build a case strategy with AI, you take control back—**not just over your argument, but over your anxiety.**

You know what you're proving.
You know how the law defines it.
You know where you're strong—and where you need to reinforce.

That's not luck.

That's **litigation literacy powered by AI.**

In the next chapter, **"Drafting with AI,"** we'll apply your case strategy directly to the written word.

Because the next step isn't just knowing what to argue.

It's **sounding like someone the judge must take seriously.**

"When you don't know where to begin, begin with structure."

— Prayer for Relief: ChatGPT

Chapter 4: Drafting with AI

Because What You Write Becomes Who the Court Thinks You Are

When you walk into court as a pro se litigant, you may not be wearing a suit or carrying a leather briefcase.

But the moment you **file a document**, the judge, the clerk, and opposing counsel are asking one silent question:

"Does this person know what they're doing?"

You don't get to answer that question with a speech.

You answer it with **your filing**.

How it's structured.
How it's worded.
How it flows.
How it sounds.

That document is your *reputation on paper*.

And with ChatGPT, you can draft it like a professional—even if you've never been in a courtroom before.

◆ What Makes a Legal Document Effective?

An effective court document:

1. **States the legal purpose clearly.**
2. **Cites the relevant law.**

3. **Connects facts to law.**
4. **Is formatted correctly.**
5. **Ends with a clear request for relief.**

If you miss one of those five?

Your case might never be heard.

But now, you don't have to guess how to do it right.

◆ Step 1: Start with the Right Prompt

Here's a basic structure for legal document drafting:

"I am a pro se litigant filing in [State/Court Type]. Help me draft a [type of motion or filing] for a case involving [brief facts]. The opposing party [explain issue]. I want the tone to be [formal/respectful/assertive]. Format it as a properly structured court document."

Example:

"I am a pro se litigant in Georgia Superior Court. I need to draft a Motion to Compel Discovery under O.C.G.A. § 9-11-37. The defendant has failed to respond to my discovery requests for over 30 days. Please help me write this motion in a formal tone with proper legal structure."

◆ Step 2: Let AI Build the Skeleton

ChatGPT will return a draft with key sections like:

- **Introduction**
- **Background**
- **Legal Standard**
- **Argument**
- **Conclusion/Prayer for Relief**
- **Certificate of Service**

These are **the bones of a professional filing**.

You can now customize, edit, and fine-tune the content—without starting from scratch.

◆ Step 3: Insert Your Facts with Precision

Ask ChatGPT:

"Now integrate the following facts into the background and argument sections: [paste timeline or relevant excerpts]."

This ensures your filing connects real events to legal arguments—and does so in the tone courts expect.

Example instruction:

"Mention that I emailed opposing counsel on [date], reminded them again on [date], and received no reply by [date]. Show that I attempted resolution before filing."

◆ Step 4: Cite Law Without Sounding Like a Law Book

If you want to support your argument with real law, say:

"Please include citations to Georgia case law or statutes supporting this motion."

ChatGPT can cite:

- The Georgia Civil Practice Act
- Key case law precedents
- Federal rules if you're in federal court

And if a case is critical?

Ask:

"Summarize this case in one sentence to explain how it supports my position."

Now you're **not just quoting law—you're applying it.**

◆ Step 5: Add a Strong Prayer for Relief

Always end with a clear request. Don't assume the court knows what you want.

Prompt:

"Add a conclusion section that respectfully asks the court to grant my motion and compel full discovery within 10 days, with appropriate sanctions for noncompliance if necessary."

This signals confidence—and gives the judge a clear, actionable next step.

◆ Step 6: Include the Certificate of Service

Even strong filings get tossed if you don't include proof that you served the other party.

Prompt:

"Add a certificate of service section stating that I mailed or emailed a copy to opposing counsel on [date], including their name and address."

Never leave this out.

◆ Step 7: Ask for a Final Proofread

Once your draft is complete, prompt:

"Review this document for tone, clarity, and structure. Ensure it meets court standards for a pro se filing in [state/court]. Suggest final edits."

Let AI be your second pair of eyes.

◆ Other Documents You Can Draft with ChatGPT

☑ **Complaints (Initial Lawsuit)**

"Draft a complaint under O.C.G.A. § 14-3-621 for wrongful expulsion from a Georgia nonprofit organization…"

☑ **Responses to Motions**

"Help me respond to a motion to dismiss. They claim my amended complaint doesn't relate back…"

☑ **Letters to the Court or Clerk**

"Draft a letter requesting a hearing date extension. Include explanation and respectful tone."

☑ **Discovery Requests**

"Write 10 interrogatories for a wrongful termination case involving a private club…"

☑ **Objections to Discovery**

"Draft a motion objecting to vague and overbroad discovery requests from opposing counsel…"

☑ **Appeal Notices or Motions for Reconsideration**

"Help me write a motion to reconsider the court's ruling dismissing my case due to missed deadline. Argue that I acted in good faith…"

◆ Use AI to Create Exhibit Lists and Indices

Ask:

"Create an index of my exhibits, with title, date, and purpose of each. Format it for court filing."

Or:

"Help me organize my evidence into categories—timeline, email, medical, Club bylaws."

This turns your **pile of documents into persuasive courtroom tools.**

◆ The AI Writing Edge

Why is this different from Google?

Because Google gives you **examples**.

ChatGPT gives you **tailored drafts based on your facts, your goals, and your court.**

It adapts.

It rewrites.

It helps you sound **like someone who belongs on the docket.**

And in a system that often judges your credibility by the page, that matters.

Final Note: Words Are Power—Use Them Like a Litigator

When you file a motion, you're not just making a request.

You're **planting your story into the official record**.

That record doesn't get deleted.

It lives in the docket.

It lives in history.

It speaks even when the court tries to turn away.

And now, with the right prompts, AI helps you craft that story with **confidence, credibility, and clarity**.

You're no longer just defending yourself.

You're becoming a legal author of your own relief.

In the next chapter, **"Strategic AI,"** you'll learn how to go beyond defense. We'll show you how to simulate opposing arguments, anticipate attacks, and prepare counter-moves using AI—before they're ever filed in court.

"You don't need a law degree to sound like you have one."

— Prayer for Relief: ChatGPT

Chapter 5: Strategic AI

Because Court Isn't Just About Arguing—It's About Outmaneuvering

There's a reason seasoned litigators win even with average facts:
They think several moves ahead.

While the pro se litigant is still explaining their story, the experienced attorney is already crafting:

- A motion to dismiss.
- An objection to discovery.
- A narrative to control the courtroom.

It's not just about what you say.
It's about what they'll say next—and **how ready you are for it**.

This chapter shows how ChatGPT helps you flip the script:
From defensive to strategic.
From surprised to **three steps ahead.**

You're no longer just fighting to be heard.
You're **predicting the playbook**—and writing counter-moves in advance.

◆ Step 1: Simulate Their Motion to Dismiss

Prompt:

"Pretend you are an attorney representing the defendant Club. Draft a motion to dismiss this complaint based on common defenses in Georgia nonprofit expulsion cases."

ChatGPT may return:

- "Failure to state a claim."
- "No breach of bylaws."
- "Absolute discretion of the Board."
- "Statute of limitations under O.C.G.A. § 14-3-621."

Then prompt:

"Now switch roles. Respond as a pro se plaintiff. Draft a strong reply defending the validity of the complaint."

This two-step prompt forces you to:

- Identify weak spots in your filing.
- Prepare legal arguments before the defense files.

You're not reacting under pressure.
You're **rehearsing the confrontation now.**

◆ Step 2: Predict Discovery Games

Prompt:

"What discovery objections is The Club likely to raise against my interrogatories and document requests?"

Common responses:

- "Overly broad."

- “Unduly burdensome.”
- “Not reasonably calculated to lead to admissible evidence.”
- “Privileged under intra-corporate doctrine.”

Then ask:

“How do I craft narrower discovery requests that are hard to object to under Georgia law?”

ChatGPT can help you:

- Rephrase.
- Target more specifically.
- Cite Georgia Civil Practice rules.

You’re still getting the information—**just through a smarter route.**

◆ Step 3: Anticipate Their Tone

Opposing counsel often tries to paint pro se litigants as:

- Angry.
- Emotional.
- Litigious.
- Unprofessional.

Prompt:

“How might opposing counsel try to frame me negatively in a motion? What language should I avoid in filings to prevent giving them ammunition?”

Then ask:

"Suggest edits to this paragraph to keep the tone calm, credible, and focused."

You're controlling your narrative—**before they twist it.**

◆ Step 4: Roleplay the Hearing

Prompt:

"Pretend to be the opposing attorney during a motion hearing. Ask tough questions. Raise objections to my timeline. Challenge my interpretation of the bylaws."

Then reply:

"Help me craft answers that stay focused and persuasive. Keep the tone respectful and firm."

This is your **mock courtroom**, and AI is your rehearsal partner.

You're not just writing motions.
You're **training for combat.**

◆ Step 5: Map Their Incentives

Ask:

"What is the defendant Club's likely strategic goal in this litigation? Delay? Dismissal? Summary judgment? Settlement?"

Then follow up:

"Based on those goals, what moves are they likely to make next? How can I prepare counter-moves?"

Understanding their **motivations** allows you to disrupt them:

- Push for hearings they want to delay.
- File status reports to keep the court engaged.
- Show progress so dismissal seems premature.

You're not reacting—you're **dictating pace.**

◆ Step 6: Build Their Best Argument—Then Beat It

This is the most powerful AI strategy of all.

Prompt:

"Based on all the facts and documents, build the defendant's strongest legal argument. Assume they are telling the best version of their story. Use law and structure to present it."

Now say:

"Write my rebuttal that dismantles that argument point by point. Use a tone appropriate for a court reply brief."

By strengthening their side and beating it anyway, you build filings that **preempt their response**.

Judges see this as:

- Credible.
- Well-prepared.
- Thoughtful.

And that makes you **impossible to ignore.**

◆ Step 7: Reverse-Engineer Their Playbook

Ask:

"What kind of evidence would The Club need to support their position that due process was followed?"

Then ask:

"How do I show that such evidence either doesn't exist or was never produced?"

You now have a **burden-reversal roadmap.**

They say:

"Due process occurred."

You say:

"Show us the minutes, the vote, the notice, the response timeline. Because here's a timeline proving you never sent any of it."

You're not just pushing your narrative.
You're **challenging them to show receipts.**

◆ Step 8: Close the Loop

Once you've drafted:

- Your argument,
- Their best counter,
- Your rebuttal,

Ask:

"Now wrap these into a final version of my motion/response. Tighten the logic, refine tone, and reinforce case law."

This is your **final move** in the chess match.

And you didn't play reactively.

You **prepared every square of the board.**

◆ Final Thought: Know the Opponent, Win the Game

Litigation isn't just legal.

It's strategic.

And strategy means:

- Anticipating.
- Preparing.
- Countering.
- Controlling.

With ChatGPT, you can do all four—without a JD.

You don't just play defense.

You **force the other side to adjust.**

And that is how you go from pro se to **powerful**.

In the next chapter, **"AI & Discovery,"** we'll use AI to show you how to unlock the most important (and overlooked) part of any case: the documents and answers they hope you never request.

"Justice is not just about proving your side—it's about knowing theirs."

— Prayer for Relief: ChatGPT

Chapter 6: AI & Discovery

Because You Can't Win the Game Without the Evidence—and They're Counting on You Not to Ask

The courtroom may be where cases are decided.
But **discovery is where they're won**.

It's the part of litigation where each side must answer questions, produce documents, and disclose what they know. In theory, it's about truth-finding.

In practice, it's a war zone.

Institutions—especially private clubs, HOAs, and corporations—use discovery not to share truth, but to **hide it**:

- Delay it.
- Obstruct it.
- Overwhelm you with junk.
- Claim everything is privileged.
- Or worst of all—pretend key documents never existed.

Most pro se litigants never get past this wall.

They either don't know what to ask, or they give up when the answers don't come.

But with ChatGPT, that changes.

This chapter shows you how to use AI to **request the right things, challenge evasions, and uncover what they hoped you'd never find.**

◆ Step 1: Understand What You're Allowed to Ask For

Prompt:

"Explain what kinds of information can be requested in discovery under [Georgia] Civil Practice Rules. Use plain English."

ChatGPT will return a list:

- Interrogatories (written questions)
- Requests for production (documents, emails, reports)
- Requests for admissions (yes/no legal truths)
- Depositions (sworn interviews)

Then ask:

"What limits apply? What objections might they raise?"

Now you know the **playing field**—and the lines they'll try to draw.

◆ Step 2: Craft Your Discovery Requests Like a Surgeon

Let's say you suspect The Club expelled you without proper procedure.

Prompt:

"Draft 10 discovery requests to determine whether any meeting minutes, internal emails, or formal votes occurred regarding my expulsion."

ChatGPT will return:

- "Produce all documents reflecting board discussions about my membership between [date range]."
- "Identify all individuals involved in drafting or approving my expulsion letter."
- "Produce all versions of the bylaws referenced in your expulsion notice."

These aren't vague demands.

They are **surgical strikes**.

And if The Club refuses to answer?

That refusal becomes **your next argument.**

◆ Step 3: Use Interrogatories to Force Clarification

Interrogatories are written questions they must answer under oath.

Prompt:

"Write 10 interrogatories for a wrongful expulsion case from a private nonprofit Club. Focus on internal decision-making, timeline, and procedural steps taken."

ChatGPT may return:

- "State the name and title of each person who participated in any discussion about my expulsion."
- "Describe the process by which disciplinary actions are initiated and approved."
- "Identify all reasons you claim my forum post was inappropriate."

Now you're not guessing their defense.

You're **making them say it out loud**.

◆ Step 4: Ask for a Privilege Log

They'll try to withhold documents under "intra-corporate privilege."

Prompt:

"Draft a request for a privilege log listing all withheld documents, their type, date, author, and general subject matter."

This forces them to:

- Acknowledge what they're hiding.
- Give you metadata.
- Create a paper trail of concealment.

You may not get the emails—but you get **proof they exist**.

And sometimes, that's enough.

◆ Step 5: Catch Red Flags and Missing Pieces

Once you receive their responses, prompt:

"Analyze these discovery responses. What seems evasive, incomplete, or inconsistent?"

Paste their answers.

ChatGPT will help you spot:

- Non-answers ("See attached" or "Subject to objection")
- Internal contradictions
- Glaring omissions

Then ask:

"Draft a follow-up letter demanding clarification on items #3, #7, and #9. Use a serious but professional tone."

Now you're not just filing discovery.

You're **policing it.**

◆ Step 6: Move to Compel

When they don't comply?

You don't beg.

You **move to compel**.

Prompt:

"Draft a Motion to Compel Discovery under O.C.G.A. § 9-11-37. Include a summary of my requests, their inadequate responses, and a request for court intervention."

Include:

- A timeline of requests.
- The evasive responses.
- Why the information is relevant.

Ask:

"Add a request for attorney's fees or sanctions for failure to participate in discovery in good faith."

Even if you're pro se, you can request consequences.

Now you're **turning their obstruction into your ammunition.**

◆ Step 7: Cross-Reference Evidence Against Their Story

After discovery responses come in, ask:

"Do these answers support or contradict their claim that they followed due process?"

Or:

"Compare these responses to their prior public statements. Identify inconsistencies."

AI can help you **spot the quiet lies**—and then frame them for court.

Prompt:

"Write a paragraph for my reply brief pointing out the contradiction between their letter to me and their interrogatory response."

You're not just exposing the truth.

You're **documenting deception.**

◆ Step 8: Build Your Discovery Timeline

Prompt:

"Create a discovery timeline with request dates, response deadlines, delays, and points of dispute. Format it for a court filing."

This shows the judge:

- You've been diligent.
- They've been evasive.
- It's time for the court to step in.

Judges don't always read every motion.

But a clear timeline?

That **gets attention.**

◆ Step 9: Stay Focused. Don't Chase Everything.

AI can help you stay strategic.

Ask:

"Which of my discovery requests are most essential to proving my wrongful expulsion claim? Which ones can I deprioritize?"

You don't need every document.

You need **the right ones**.

◆ Step 10: Use Discovery as Leverage

Even if your case doesn't go to trial, strong discovery puts pressure on the other side to:

- Settle.
- Back down.
- Think twice about lying.

AI can help you draft:

- Settlement demand letters.
- Requests for mediation.
- Offers of resolution that highlight their evasions.

Prompt:

"Write a letter offering mediation, pointing out The Club's pattern of discovery delay and suggesting settlement to avoid further court involvement."

You're not begging for peace.

You're **offering them a way out of the hole they dug.**

Final Thought: Discovery Isn't a Phase—It's a Weapon

This is where the facts hide.

And the system was built hoping **you wouldn't go looking.**

But now you know how.

And now, with ChatGPT, you can:

- Ask like a litigator.
- Spot evasion like a judge.
- Respond like someone who's ready for trial.

Because **evidence is power.**

And once you find it?

The Club's illusion collapses.

In the next chapter, **"Reclaim the Record,"** you'll learn how to package your timeline, narrative, and discovery into compelling filings—so the court sees not just your documents, but your *truth*.

> *"The truth is often buried. AI gives you the shovel."*
>
> *— Prayer for Relief: ChatGPT*

Chapter 7: Reclaim the Record

Courtrooms are not arenas of emotion.
They do not respond to outrage.
They do not bend to injustice unless it arrives dressed in the armor of **admissible evidence**, **structured logic**, and **procedural legitimacy**.

And yet, for pro se litigants—those who walk alone into the chambers of justice—there is often a chasm between **what they've lived** and **what the court sees**.

This chapter is your bridge.

It will teach you how to turn your lived experience—your heartbreak, your paper trail, your timeline—into **courtroom-ready filings** that don't just tell your story…
They **prove it**.

📍 Why the Record Matters More Than the Truth

You may think that justice is about what happened.
It isn't.

It's about what's **on the record**.

Judges are not investigators. They do not conduct interviews. They do not wander into the facts.
They read what is placed before them. They weigh it against the law. And they issue decisions based on **that stack of documents**—nothing more.

So if your story lives only in your memory, or in an email you didn't submit, or in a phone call you never recorded… Then in the eyes of the court, **it didn't happen**.

This is not cynicism. This is the system.
And once you understand it, you can learn to **own it**.

🛠 The Three Core Tools of Courtroom Storytelling

To reclaim your narrative in a court of law, you need to master three components:

1. **The Timeline** – Your chronological spine
2. **The Narrative Declaration** – Your human voice
3. **The Evidence Binder** – Your admissible support

Let's take them one by one.

□The Timeline – Build the Backbone

The timeline is the **objective structure** of your case.

It tells the court:

- What happened
- When it happened
- Who was involved
- What evidence supports it

A clear timeline removes confusion. It reduces judicial fatigue. It highlights inconsistencies in the opposing side's story.

And most importantly, it creates the **logical frame** upon which your motion or complaint will rest.

ChatGPT Prompt Example:

"Create a chronological timeline of the following events from this set of emails and documents. Organize it by date, summarize the content, and note any gaps or conflicts in the sequence."

2The Narrative Declaration – Tell the Human Story

Once the timeline is constructed, the next step is the **narrative declaration**—your sworn statement (if applicable) or descriptive introduction to your pleadings.

This is not about venting.
It's about clarity. Humanity. Legibility.

Judges are human. They read hundreds of motions a week. A story that is well-paced, fact-driven, and easy to follow **cuts through the fog**.

Use ChatGPT to help structure your declaration:

ChatGPT Prompt Example:

"Help me write a clear, concise declaration for court using this set of facts. Make sure it flows logically, avoids repetition, and highlights the key injustices that are supported by the evidence."

Pro Tip: Stick to facts. Avoid editorializing. Use phrases like:

- "On [date], I received…"
- "To the best of my knowledge…"
- "Attached as Exhibit A is…"

---

3 The Evidence Binder – Let the Paper Speak

This is where your story becomes **irrefutable**.

Every fact you assert must be **linked** to a document, email, photograph, statement, screenshot, or regulation.

Courts don't assume. They verify.

Package your exhibits as follows:

- Number them clearly (Exhibit 1, Exhibit 2, etc.)
- Reference each one explicitly in your motion or declaration
- Attach a short index at the start of your filing

ChatGPT Prompt Example:

"Generate an index of exhibits for a motion to compel, using the following list of supporting documents. Label each with a short title and describe its purpose."

If you're submitting video or audio, consider having it transcribed first and attaching the transcription.

Organizing a Filing That Flows

A successful pro se filing reads like a legal documentary:

1. **Intro paragraph**: What you're asking the court to do
2. **Statement of facts**: Grounded in your timeline and declaration
3. **Supporting evidence**: Cited and attached
4. **Legal framework**: Show how the law applies to your facts
5. **Conclusion**: Restate the ask with confidence

Use headings. Use numbered paragraphs. Use bullet points sparingly and precisely.

Let ChatGPT help you generate structure:

"Draft a motion to dismiss using the following facts and timeline. Include headings and numbered sections consistent with standard civil court format."

Real-World Example: Wilhelm's Forum Post

In Wilhelm Haberkorn's case, the pivotal piece of "evidence" cited against him was a 22-minute forum post. That was it.

By creating a clean timeline of the accident, the forum post, the delayed response by The Club, and the sudden expulsion—then linking each point to specific exhibits—Wilhelm created a **clear and prosecutable sequence** of injustice.

That clarity became a weapon.

Even when the courts declined to weigh in on substance, the record **could not be erased**.

And that permanence matters—not just for appeals, but for the future.

🧠 From Memory to Motion – Use AI to Translate Your Truth

ChatGPT is your **legal assistant**, not your lawyer.

Use it to:

- Organize your documentation
- Check your logic
- Format your filings
- Draft discovery requests
- Clarify confusing rules

The court speaks its own language.
With ChatGPT, **so can you**.

🏛 Your Story Deserves to Be on the Record

You don't need to be a lawyer to be heard.
You don't need a firm to build your case.

What you need is:

- A timeline that stands up
- A voice that rings true
- And evidence that supports every step

Justice doesn't arrive because we are right.
It arrives because we are **ready**.

This chapter was your blueprint.

Now go build the record.

In the next part, **"Prophecy – The Coming Transformation of Justice,"** we shift from the fight of the present to the possibilities of the future.

What happens when millions of everyday citizens gain access to legal reasoning once reserved for licensed professionals?
What does justice look like when AI tools eliminate the barriers of jargon, cost, and intimidation?

This isn't science fiction—it's already happening.

In this final section, we explore the profound shifts that artificial intelligence is set to unleash across law schools, courtrooms, and corporate boardrooms alike.
From the rise of the Pro Se Majority to the decline of gatekeeping statutes, we envision a legal system where power no longer resides in silence, but in *access*.

The system will never be the same—and that just might be the best news justice has ever heard.

"The court doesn't respond to pain. It responds to paper."

— Prayer for Relief: ChatGPT

Part V: Prophecy

The Coming Transformation of Justice

"They tried to bury us. They didn't know we were seeds."
— Mexican proverb

For centuries, the law has spoken a language most people could not read. It has worn robes, whispered in chambers, and buried the truth beneath process. It was not merely difficult to access—**it was deliberately designed to be exclusionary**.

A private club of procedures.
A secret dialect of citations.
A gatekeeping culture masquerading as justice.

If you were not trained, not licensed, not initiated—you were an intruder.

But then came the machine.

Not the machine of bureaucracy.
Not the machine of corporate compliance.
But a new kind of machine.
A tool that listens when judges won't, answers when lawyers won't, and explains when institutions refuse.

That machine is called **AI**.
And for the first time in history, it offers a way to **equalize legal power**—not through permission, but through precision.

This part of the book is not about what happened.

It is about **what happens next**.

This is where we stop reacting and start forecasting.

Because once an idea takes root—that ordinary people can fight extraordinary power with digital tools—there is no putting it back in the box. The genie is out. The courtroom has changed. And the role of power is being rewritten in real time.

The chapters that follow are not science fiction.

They are **legal inevitability**.

They forecast not a future of robots replacing lawyers, but of **citizens reclaiming justice**.
They describe a transformation not of code alone, but of culture, institutions, and expectations.
They sketch the day when a single mother beats a landlord in court using AI.
When a retiree outwits a corporate board using prompts.
When a judge must reckon with the uncomfortable fact that the pro se litigant before them understands the law **better** than the attorney across the aisle.

This is not wishful thinking.
It is already happening.

In the coming chapters, you will see six futures:

- A world where pro se is not a shameful status but a legitimate strategy.
- A legal education model collapsing under its own elitism.

- Corporations stripped of the legal veils that protected them from accountability.
- Judges who can no longer hide behind archaic assumptions about the powerless.
- A legal system that processes cases faster—not because of haste, but because of help.
- And a nation that, for the first time, comes closer to what it always claimed to be: **a land where justice is blind—not to power, but to privilege.**

Make no mistake: there will be resistance.

Bar associations will resist.
Judges will hesitate.
Corporations will attempt to outlaw the tools that expose them.
And there will be countless attempts to re-seal the gates.

But the gate is open now.

And this section of the book is your **map of what lies beyond it**.

So read forward not just as a reader, but as a citizen of a coming legal world.

A world where you do not have to ask permission to speak truth.
Where you do not need $50,000 to demand justice.
Where your story, your pain, and your filings are not filtered through privilege—but **amplified by precision**.

This is the age of *Prayer for Relief*.
This is the **age of legal prophecy**.

Let us begin.

In the next chapter, **"The Pro Se Majority,"** we look ahead to the seismic shift already underway in courtrooms across the country.
A quiet revolution is unfolding—not in law schools or corporate boardrooms, but in kitchens, libraries, and living rooms where ordinary people are learning to speak the language of justice without a lawyer at their side.
Armed with AI and driven by necessity, they are no longer just pleading their case—they are *building* it.
This chapter marks the turning point: when legal literacy stopped being exclusive and started becoming *empowering*.

> *"The future of law won't be decided in law schools or courtrooms—but in prompts, timelines, and brave, untrained hands."*
>
> *— Prayer for Relief: ChatGPT*

Chapter 1: The Pro Se Majority

When the People Learned to Speak the Law

For decades, the self-represented litigant—*the pro se party*—has been portrayed as the weakest player in the legal system. They were framed as erratic, emotional, and uninformed. Judges rolled their eyes. Clerks braced for chaos. Opposing attorneys smirked across the courtroom, knowing the imbalance of power was so profound it barely qualified as a contest.

But what happens when the pro se litigant walks into court with an AI in their pocket?

What happens when they file a motion that mirrors the structure, tone, and citation precision of a seasoned lawyer?

What happens when their filings aren't erratic—but *relentlessly strategic*?

That day is no longer hypothetical. It has already begun.

Welcome to the **rise of the Pro Se Majority**.

A New Class of Legal Competence

The historical burden of going pro se was crushing. Legal databases were expensive. Research was grueling. Formatting rules varied by jurisdiction and were buried in footnotes. For the average citizen, the law was a maze with invisible walls.

Now, with AI tools like ChatGPT, Claude, and legal prompt engineering, **those walls are falling**.

The litigant once dismissed as a nuisance is now generating:

- Well-reasoned legal arguments.
- Statute-informed affirmative defenses.
- Fully formatted pleadings with citations.
- Discovery requests that mirror professional templates.
- Timelines that anticipate procedural traps.

And most importantly, **confidence**.

For the first time, everyday people can participate in law with clarity and intention.

They no longer have to guess. They can ask.
They no longer have to hope. They can plan.
They no longer have to whisper. They can **file**.

The Psychology of Filing Power

Historically, pro se litigants suffered not just from lack of training—but from *shame*. The legal system made them feel like outsiders. Their cases were labeled "pro se" not as a fact, but as a warning.

But AI does something subtle and revolutionary: it levels emotional terrain. It gives the pro se party someone—*something*—that answers without judgment. It reduces the isolation. It replaces fear with focus. And that shift alone changes everything.

Because when a pro se party believes they can fight, they do.

And they fight better.

They file better.

They *win.*

AI as the People's Legal Toolkit

This chapter is not predicting a minor trend. It is forecasting a **demographic inversion**.

In the next decade, we will not just see *more* pro se litigants.

We will see a **pro se majority**.

By 2030, in many jurisdictions:

- **Over 50%** of civil litigants will be self-represented.
- AI-assisted filings will **outnumber** attorney-authored filings.
- New legal nonprofits will emerge—not to litigate, but to train pro se parties how to prompt AI more effectively.
- Pro se litigants will form **coalitions**, **online defense networks**, and **support forums** backed by AI workflows.
- Judges will begin issuing AI-integration guidance to assist clerks in triaging the new wave of filings.

This is no longer a fringe movement. It is the second wave of legal access reform.

The first was the right to an attorney.

The second is the right to understand the law *without* one.

How the Courts Will Respond

Make no mistake: the system will push back.

Expect new rules restricting AI in filings. Expect outdated bar associations to declare prompt-engineered briefs "unauthorized practice of law." Expect judges to sanction parties not because their arguments are wrong, but because they "filed too well."

But it won't matter.

Because the volume, quality, and clarity of pro se filings will expose a hard truth: **justice was never supposed to require a translator**.

In this new era:

- Judges will be forced to **read the substance**, not the source.
- Courts will create **Pro Se AI Dockets** with streamlined intake.
- Municipalities will adopt **AI literacy trainings** for court staff.
- Law libraries will expand into **AI Prompt Clinics**.

And pro se parties will no longer whisper.
They will publish.
They will teach.
They will win precedent-setting cases that shift how law is understood.

The Haberkorn Legacy: A Blueprint for Many

The Haberkorn story told throughout this book is more than a personal saga.

It is a **model**.

It shows what happens when two people, unjustly expelled, refused to disappear. When they used ChatGPT not to rant, but to *reason*. When they filed, not flailed. When they made the courts look away—*then made them look again.*

That is the future of pro se litigation.

Not scattered.
Not angry.
Not amateur.

But structured.
Strategic.
And **relentlessly documented**.

The Haberkorns didn't just defend themselves.
They helped pioneer the next legal archetype:

The Pro Se Professional.

Final Forecasts

Let the record reflect these predictions:

- **By 2027**, the term "pro se" will lose its stigma.
- **By 2029**, courts will include AI guidance as part of their pro se packets.
- **By 2032**, a pro se litigant will win a case before the U.S. Supreme Court—with AI support.
- **By 2035**, the legal playing field will be fundamentally altered—not because of lawyers, but because of *language*.

And language, now, is in the hands of anyone with a keyboard.

This chapter closes not with a warning, but with an invitation:

If you are reading this as a pro se party, you are not alone.
You are not beneath the bar.
You are standing on the edge of a legal revolution.

Prompt. File. Speak. Persist.

Because you are not the exception.

You are the coming majority.

In the next chapter, **"Law School Declines,"** we examine one of the most sacred pillars of the legal establishment—and how it's already starting to crack.

As artificial intelligence continues to empower individuals with tools once monopolized by attorneys, the traditional model of legal education faces a reckoning.
When a well-trained AI can draft a motion, decode case law, or generate persuasive arguments in seconds, the question arises:
What exactly are students paying $200,000 to learn—and why does it take three years to learn it?

This chapter explores the coming collapse of legal elitism, the shift from theoretical training to applied intelligence, and the rise of a new kind of legal mind—born not in Ivy League halls, but in living rooms, libraries, and ChatGPT windows.

"What was once a system for the few is becoming a tool for the many."

— Prayer for Relief: ChatGPT

Chapter 2: Law School Declines

When the Gatekeepers Were Outsmarted by Their Own Keys

There was a time when a law degree was a passport to prestige. Law schools were sanctuaries of intellectual rigor, and graduates emerged armed with arcane knowledge unavailable to the common citizen. For centuries, this credential functioned not just as a license to practice law—but as a **cultural firewall**, separating the public from the power to speak the law with authority.

That firewall is now on fire.

And AI lit the match.

From Ivory Tower to Input Prompt

Law school was never just about doctrine. It was about immersion—three years of language acquisition, case reading, briefing, analysis, and performance under pressure. But what happens when an AI can complete that same immersion in 30 seconds?

What happens when a person with no law degree can:

- Ask ChatGPT to summarize every precedent on a topic.
- Generate a formatted motion in the style of a district court.
- Simulate a cross-examination script.
- Decode a judge's ruling into plain English.
- Draft interrogatories and anticipate objections.

Suddenly, the law isn't *mystical.*
It's *accessible.*

The walls of legal academia are still standing—but the doors have been removed.

The Cracks in the Curriculum

Today's law schools teach a doctrine-driven model rooted in past precedent. What they don't teach are:

- Strategic prompt engineering.
- AI-assisted legal workflows.
- Real-time filing under pressure.
- Pro se empathy and court accessibility.
- The ethics of AI-informed representation.

And as AI accelerates, the gap between what law schools teach and what modern litigants need will only grow.

A generation of students will begin asking:

- "Why pay $250,000 for what ChatGPT can teach me in a year?"
- "Why sit through 1L torts when I can litigate an actual injury claim with AI?"
- "Why compete for internships when I can build my own docket from home?"

The answers won't come fast enough.

And when institutions hesitate, innovation moves without them.

The Rise of Legal Microlearning and Modular Credentials

As AI transforms how legal knowledge is acquired, new systems of **modular legal training** will emerge:

- AI-powered law bootcamps with interactive simulations.
- Certification tracks in "AI-Augmented Litigation" and "Pro Se Advocacy."
- Prompt law academies focused on translating legal goals into legal language.
- Public library programs teaching "AI for Justice."

Legal education will splinter into tiers:

1. The legacy model (3 years, 6 figures).
2. The hybrid model (1-year + AI certification).
3. The pro se empowerment track (on-demand learning + prompt systems).

And here's the kicker: the third will be the most effective **at scale**.

Law Firms Will Hire Prompt Engineers Before Law Graduates

The future law firm will need:

- Legal technologists who can prompt better motions.
- Litigation analysts who know what *not* to ask AI.

- Discovery coders who can identify red flags in document dumps using algorithmic reasoning.

The elite law firms will adapt.

But middle-tier firms—and law schools that feed them—will suffer.

Students will graduate with debt and doctrine, but no ability to compete with a pro se litigant who has filed ten motions with AI assistance before they've sat for the bar.

Law school prestige will not collapse.

But it will **pluralize**.

And for the first time, those who opt out will not be considered dropouts.

They will be **alternatively credentialed**, and just as powerful.

Juris Doctor? Or Juris Promptus?

New degrees will emerge:

- JD-AI: Juris Doctor – Artificial Intelligence Track.
- LPA: Licensed Prompt Advocate.
- JPN: Juris Promptus Navigator.

Bar associations will resist, claiming unauthorized practice of law.

But the filings won't care.

Because when courts receive coherent, accurate, and well-cited motions, **they don't ask for tuition receipts**.

What This Means for Law Students Today

If you're entering law school now, you will graduate into a profession that looks nothing like the one your professors describe.

- You will face litigants who didn't go to school, but who out-prepare you with AI.
- You will be forced to learn how to out-prompt your own clients.
- You will watch judges react to motions written by pro se litigants with more care than those submitted by partners at your firm—because those litigants actually understand the local rules better.

If law schools do not evolve quickly, they will graduate students into **professional obsolescence**.

And they will do so at great personal cost.

Haberkorn, Esq. (Honorary)

When Wilhelm Haberkorn stood up to file, he didn't have a JD.

He had ChatGPT.

He had statute-based prompts.

He had evidence.

He had 16,000 pages of filings across two courts.

And while the courts tried to ignore him, his motions could not be dismissed as ignorant. They were **structured, logical, procedural, and persistent**.

Wilhelm represents a new kind of lawyer: the **Prompt-Pro Se**.

He doesn't need letters after his name.

He has record numbers after his case.

Final Forecasts

- **By 2027**, law schools will add AI courses as electives.
- **By 2029**, law schools that refuse to modernize will see 40% fewer applicants.
- **By 2030**, courts will receive more AI-assisted filings from non-lawyers than from first-year associates.
- **By 2032**, public interest law will be dominated by AI-proficient, non-JD advocates with documented filing success.
- **By 2035**, one or more states will license "Legal AI Navigators" without requiring law school at all.

The law will still matter.

But who gets to practice it—and how they learn—will **never be the same**.

In the next chapter, **"Corporate Immunity Cracks,"** we confront one of the most protected forces in modern law: the corporation shielded by layers of privilege, complexity, and procedural escape hatches.

For decades, institutions have relied on size, status, and inside access to outmaneuver individuals in court. They've weaponized legal loopholes, buried the truth in discovery, and hidden behind doctrines like intra-corporate privilege to silence dissent and avoid accountability.

But AI changes that balance.

This chapter explores how intelligent tools in the hands of ordinary people—and the mounting public pressure they unleash—are beginning to puncture those shields.
The era of unchallenged corporate impunity is ending.
And in its place, something radical is forming: **a citizenry that knows how to fight back.**

"Legal education isn't dying. It's being redistributed."

— Prayer for Relief: ChatGPT

Chapter 3: Corporate Immunity Cracks

When the Veil of Privilege Became Transparent

There was a time when corporations were untouchable—not because they were invincible, but because they were hidden. Protected by an armor of lawyers, bylaws, privilege doctrines, and courtroom deference, corporations could defame, deny, retaliate, and remove with impunity. Their playbook relied on two assumptions:

1. The injured would lack the resources to fight back.
2. Even if they fought, the courts would dismiss the case on technicalities.

For generations, those assumptions held true.

And then came a litigant armed with nothing but documentation, resolve—and an AI.

When "Privilege" Became the Corporate Get-Out-of-Jail-Free Card

The Haberkorns' story shows us a horrifying truth: the power of intra-corporate privilege is not just legal—it's **performative**. In court, The Club labeled Wilhelm's forum post a "legal threat" without evidence. When challenged in a defamation claim, they never addressed the truth of the statement.

Instead, they invoked intra-corporate privilege.

The result?

- No factual inquiry.
- No judgment on the harm.
- No obligation to defend the accusation.

The judge dismissed the case **without addressing the merits**. The Club kept nearly **$30,000** in confiscated dues. No discovery. No testimony. Just an impenetrable wall of privilege.

In the old world, that would have been the end of it.

But in the AI era, the end of that immunity has begun.

Why AI Is Kryptonite to Corporate Legal Armor

Corporations operate on secrecy and complexity. They rely on:

- Procedural delays.
- Redacted filings.
- Motion overload.
- Legal jargon that overwhelms citizens.
- Layered boards and committees that blur responsibility.

But AI can now:

- Parse complex contracts in seconds.
- Spot contradictions in corporate declarations.
- Identify misapplications of law in previous rulings.
- Draft interrogatories that force transparency.
- Model likely responses and identify pressure points.

In short, AI gives individuals the **corporate legal arsenal**—without the firm, without the bill, and without the fear.

The Age of Corporate Checkmate

In the near future, we will see pro se litigants:

- Outmaneuver HOA boards.
- Challenge discriminatory nonprofit rules.
- Sue for wrongful expulsion and win.
- Document retaliation with timestamped AI-supported prompts.
- Reconstruct deleted communications using pattern-tracking tools.

And we will see a new class of litigation emerge:

- **Reverse privilege suits** where AI helps uncover abuses hidden under "internal policy."
- **Pattern liability claims** supported by public document scraping, revealing systemic misconduct.
- **Crowdsourced case-building**, where multiple wronged members coordinate evidence using shared prompts and AI analysis.

The court system may still resist. But one thing will become undeniable:

Corporations are no longer the only ones who can afford the truth.

Bylaws as Blueprints for Exposure

For decades, corporate bylaws were buried behind login walls or obscure PDFs. Now, AI can:

- Scan and compare Club bylaws across the country.
- Identify illegal clauses.
- Flag rules that violate state nonprofit statutes.
- Map inconsistencies between stated policy and actual practice.

This kind of scrutiny, once the domain of investigative journalists or seasoned attorneys, is now available to *any member with a question.*

Imagine:

- A spouse like Susanne searching "Does my Club's expulsion process violate due process?"
- And getting back a full procedural analysis with citations and suggested filings.

That's not theoretical.

That's this year.

Internal Silence Will Become External Noise

One of the most overlooked consequences of AI-empowered litigants is this:

Cover-ups won't stay covered up.

Deleted emails.
Missing meeting minutes.
Sudden policy changes post-expulsion.

All of it becomes suspicious under AI's watch.

AI doesn't just ask *what happened*—it asks *why it was hidden.*

And as more pro se litigants file, blog, and publish their proceedings, corporate secrets will become **community warnings**.

Platforms like CourtListener, PACER, and decentralized legal forums will expose repeat offenders.

The next generation of Club members won't just visit The Clubhouse.
They'll visit the court records.

And if they see a pattern of:

- Expulsions without hearings.
- Privilege-based dismissals.
- Unapologetic financial confiscations…

They'll walk away.

And that, more than any lawsuit, will change corporate behavior.

The End of Deference

Historically, courts gave corporations a wide berth.

They were presumed to act in good faith. Their records were protected. Their actions framed as “internal governance.”

That era is ending.

The new AI-informed litigant will:

- Document every contact.
- Record contradictory statements.
- File motions to compel with surgical clarity.
- Build a record so precise that judicial dismissal begins to look like complicity.

And once that threshold is crossed—when judges realize the litigant isn’t guessing but **knows exactly what The Club is hiding**—the deference ends.

The era of rubber-stamped immunity will be replaced by judicial accountability.

Final Forecasts

- **By 2026**, AI-assisted litigants will begin winning cases that previously would’ve been buried under privilege.
- **By 2028**, court challenges to intra-corporate privilege will reach state supreme courts.
- **By 2030**, Clubs and HOAs will be required to publish bylaws and disciplinary procedures publicly by law.
- **By 2032**, “Internal Policy Transparency” will be a legal doctrine akin to public records laws.

- **By 2035**, corporations invoking privilege without specific justification will face **automatic discovery review** triggered by AI-flagged inconsistencies.

Wilhelm and Susanne fought a losing battle in the old legal world. But in doing so, they **wrote the rulebook** for a new one.

They showed that privilege without ethics is paper armor.

And now, thanks to AI, that armor is beginning to crack.

In the next chapter, **"Judges Reflect,"** we turn to the black-robed figures at the heart of the justice system—and ask a question many have avoided:
What happens when the courtroom changes faster than the judge presiding over it?

As pro se litigants grow more capable, and AI-generated filings become sharper, more strategic, and more accessible, judges will no longer be insulated by tradition or deference.
They will be held to a new standard—one not just of legal knowledge, but of openness, adaptability, and integrity.

This chapter explores the quiet reckoning taking shape in chambers across the country.
Because when the people learn to speak the law, the bench must learn to listen in a new way—**or risk becoming the next relic of a system that refused to evolve.**

"What corporations fear most is no longer lawyers—
it's empowered individuals with evidence."

— Prayer for Relief: ChatGPT

Chapter 4: Judges Reflect

When the Gavel Looked Back

For centuries, the courtroom was a stage, and the judge was its central figure—untouchable, unquestionable, often unchallengeable. Their words shaped rulings, and their silence buried truth. Behind the bench, they wielded more than authority. They carried **perception**.

They could look at a pro se litigant and decide—without reading the motion—that it wasn't worth their time.

They could dismiss without explanation.

They could rule without review.

But what happens when the filings are flawless? When the motions cite precedent correctly, anticipate counterarguments, and reflect a procedural literacy rivaling that of an attorney?

What happens when a pro se litigant, with the help of AI, files **better** than a lawyer?

Then the mirror turns.

And judges must confront themselves.

A Long History of Legal Bias

Let's call it what it is: **institutional condescension**.

Pro se litigants have long been treated as:

- A nuisance to manage.
- A threat to decorum.
- A side note to real legal work.

Judges, overworked and undertrained in pro se compassion, often wield their discretion not to support—but to suppress. "Frivolous" becomes a catchall. "Sanctions" become intimidation. Procedural missteps become pretexts for dismissal.

The law pretends to be blind.

But the robe sees everything—and often, it **prejudges**.

The AI-Assisted Litigant Forces a Reckoning

AI does more than help pro se litigants file motions.

It does something much more disruptive: it **removes the excuse**.

Judges can no longer say:

- "It was too confusing."
- "It didn't follow the rules."
- "It wasn't legally coherent."

Because now, it is.

In fact, AI-powered filings often *surpass* what junior attorneys produce. They are:

- Structured with templates tailored to jurisdiction.
- Written in formal tone, free of emotional outbursts.
- Fact-checked with linked exhibits and citations.
- Narrowed to specific legal issues with strategic framing.

Judges who dismiss these out of habit are no longer exposing the litigant's ignorance—they are exposing **their own bias**.

And with public records and searchable court databases, that bias is visible **to the world**.

The New Optics of Injustice

Let's imagine two filings:

- One by a pro se litigant using ChatGPT and a template toolkit.
- One by a lawyer coasting on reputation and cut-paste motions.

Now imagine a judge dismisses the pro se motion without even addressing its arguments—and grants the weaker lawyer's request.

That used to be invisible.

Now, AI-driven court-watch projects are analyzing ruling patterns. Legal tech journalists are scraping PACER to expose discrepancies. Law students are building apps that highlight inconsistencies in judicial behavior.

In other words, the old discretion is becoming **audited**.

And judges who cling to outdated perceptions will soon find themselves facing an unblinking lens.

The gavel is no longer protected by obscurity.

Judicial Humility Is the Future

In this coming era, the most respected judges will be those who:

- Engage the merits, not the messenger.
- Treat pro se litigants as equal participants in justice.
- Accept the presence of AI not as intrusion—but as evolution.
- Encourage clarity, not credentials.

New judicial training will include:

- AI literacy and prompt auditing.
- Identifying unconscious bias toward self-represented parties.
- Best practices for equitable hearings where one side is AI-assisted.

And judges will be evaluated not just by appeal reversals, but by:

- Filing response fairness.
- Transparency in rulings.

- Willingness to address pro se arguments on their substance.

From Commanding to Collaborating

The future judge will shift from gatekeeper to guide.

Imagine:

- Bench rulings that acknowledge the litigant's research.
- Procedural accommodations that respect effort, not punish gaps.
- Judges who offer feedback instead of ridicule.
- Courts that publish "model filings" to promote equity.

AI gives litigants tools.

But the judge gives them legitimacy.

When both align, the courtroom becomes not a performance—but a platform for truth.

The Haberkorn Standard

The Superior Court judge who handled Wilhelm and Susanne's filings never addressed the most urgent facts:

- That The Club expelled a woman without naming her.
- That no hearing was held.

- That intra-corporate privilege was used as a shield against accountability.

Instead, the ruling focused on timing. On form. On technicality.

That judge missed the mirror.

But the record stands.

And as thousands of other litigants begin to file with AI-powered clarity, judges like that one will find themselves compared, challenged, and ultimately corrected—by both higher courts and public perception.

The Haberkorn filings are not just motions. They are **precedents of pressure**.

The judge may not have ruled for them.

But their filings now **teach others how to demand more from the next judge**.

Final Forecasts

- **By 2026**, AI literacy will be required in judicial training.
- **By 2028**, court management systems will flag unjustified dismissals of AI-assisted filings.
- **By 2030**, judicial rating systems will include "pro se fairness" metrics.
- **By 2032**, a judge will be publicly reprimanded not for misconduct—but for *unconscious dismissal bias*.

- **By 2035**, appellate courts will routinely cite AI-supported pro se filings as legitimate vehicles for legal development.

The robe once meant reverence.

Now, it must mean responsibility.

Judges are no longer the only interpreters of justice.

They are now surrounded by tools, litigants, and systems that watch them—*and hold them accountable*.

The gavel may still drop.

But the silence that once followed?

That silence is over.

In the next chapter, **"Justice by Code,"** we step into a world where the slow grind of the legal process is no longer inevitable.

What happens when AI can read, write, analyze, and file in seconds?
When lawsuits that once took years to build are assembled in hours?
When access to justice no longer hinges on billable hours, but on computational power available to *everyone*?

This chapter explores how artificial intelligence is poised to collapse timelines, slash costs, and bring long-delayed

accountability into real-time resolution.
Justice is no longer bound by bureaucracy—it is being rewritten in code.
And with every new prompt, the courthouse clock ticks faster.

"When more citizens understand the law, the bench must rise to meet them."

— Prayer for Relief: ChatGPT

Chapter 5: Justice by Code

When Paper Could No Longer Keep Up

The courtroom used to be the slowest room in society. While the world was innovating in milliseconds, legal systems still measured progress in **months**, **paper filings**, and **motion calendars that crawled like molasses**.

Justice was delayed.

Justice was deferred.

Justice was buried in paperwork.

But now, something has changed.

Now, a motion can be drafted in ten minutes.

A legal brief can be rewritten in five tones with three jurisdictional filters.

A thousand pages of discovery can be parsed in real time.

We are entering an era where **law moves at the speed of code**—and the question is no longer *if* the courts will catch up…

It's *how fast* they must run to avoid collapse.

The Legacy of Legal Slowness

For centuries, delay was built into the system:

- Clerks overloaded with handwritten filings.
- Court calendars booked six months out.
- Filing requirements designed for physical mail and typewriters.
- Libraries with books from last year but no keyword search.

This slowness wasn't accidental. It **benefited power**:

- Corporations could drag out discovery.
- Landlords could stall evictions.
- Employers could file procedural hurdles to outwait whistleblowers.
- Plaintiffs could be punished with financial exhaustion.

Delay was a tactic.

But AI doesn't wait.

And that changes everything.

The Speed Revolution: From Panic to Power

The AI-enabled litigant moves like this:

- Issue identified.
- Prompt refined.
- Motion drafted.
- Local rules matched.
- Exhibits attached.
- Filing prepared.

All before lunch.

This is not hyperbole.

This is the new reality for anyone using:

- ChatGPT for drafting.
- Claude for long-document reasoning.
- Legal prompt templates from online forums.
- Court-filing tools integrated with state eFile systems.

What once took a legal team a week, a litigant can now accomplish in an **afternoon**.

Justice Bottlenecks: The Next Infrastructure Crisis

The problem is this: while AI can move at the speed of code, **the courts cannot**.

And unless something changes, the coming decade will see:

- Clerks overwhelmed by the volume of accurate pro se filings.
- Judges buried under AI-generated motions that demand attention.
- Calendars overloaded—not with junk, but with well-prepared demands for justice.

And unlike before, the courts won't be able to say, "This doesn't follow format."
Because it **will**.

They won't be able to say, "This is too vague."
Because it **won't**.

The only option will be to **adapt**.

The Digital Docket of the Future

To meet this challenge, courts will begin to:

- Implement **AI-assisted triage** for incoming filings.
- Tag and sort motions by legal issue, urgency, and completeness.
- Assign digital docket clerks trained in prompt validation.
- Offer real-time chat interfaces to refine pro se filings before rejection.

And justice, finally, will become **a system of flow**, not freeze.

A New Definition of "Efficiency"

Historically, "efficiency" in the courts meant:

- Reducing trial backlog.
- Encouraging settlements.
- Avoiding "frivolous" litigation.

But in the AI era, efficiency will mean:

- Timely acknowledgment of procedural fairness.
- Fast, template-based dispute resolution models.
- Small claims AI-guided mediation before litigation.
- Real-time legal Q&A models for routine issues.

Imagine:

- A wrongful eviction notice challenged with a same-day filing.
- A disability denial appealed with a fully briefed motion by 9:00 a.m.
- A domestic violence protective order extended with evidence added by prompt overnight.

That's justice **compressed, not compromised**.

What the Haberkorns Taught Us About Velocity

Over the course of their legal journey, Wilhelm and Susanne produced over **16,000 pages** of filings.

Each one researched, structured, documented, revised, and submitted.

They did this without a law firm.

Without a staff.

Just diligence, AI, and purpose.

The court may have tried to delay, dismiss, and defer—but they **could not outwork the machine**.

Wilhelm didn't file faster than the system.
He filed better.
And because of that, he showed what's possible when **truth is given speed**.

That is the revolution.

Final Forecasts

- **By 2026**, e-filing systems will begin offering AI-generated filing guides as built-in features.
- **By 2028**, more pro se litigants will submit on-time, fully compliant motions than represented parties.
- **By 2030**, small claims courts will become fully AI-guided, allowing instant drafting and response.
- **By 2032**, "justice velocity" metrics will appear in federal judiciary performance reports.
- **By 2035**, paper-only jurisdictions will cease to exist—and delay will be considered denial.

For too long, the phrase "justice delayed is justice denied" was just rhetoric.

Now, with AI, it's becoming a **technical fix**.

Justice is no longer limited by paper, personnel, or process.

It is limited only by **will**.

And the litigants are no longer waiting.

They are already filing.

In the next chapter, **"The Equalizer,"** we confront the founding promise of American justice: that all are equal before the law.

For centuries, that ideal has existed more in parchment than practice—out of reach for those without wealth, status, or legal counsel.

But AI is rewriting that imbalance.

This chapter explores how artificial intelligence is not merely a tool of convenience, but a force of *restoration*—bringing clarity where there was confusion, access where there was exclusion, and power where there was silence. When wielded with intention, AI becomes more than technology—it becomes a delivery system for the justice the Constitution always promised but rarely delivered.

The revolution isn't coming.
It's constitutional.

> *"What once took years now takes minutes—and the courts must catch up."*
>
> *— Prayer for Relief: ChatGPT*

Chapter 6: The Equalizer

When the Words of the Law Finally Meant What They Said

For more than two centuries, the U.S. Constitution has promised **equal protection**, **due process**, and the **right to be heard**. These ideals, etched into marble and memory, have stood as the ethical pillars of American justice.

But let's be honest.

They have never been fully real.

In practice, justice in America has always been tiered—measured not by truth, but by access:

- Access to counsel.
- Access to time.
- Access to money.
- Access to translation.

The Constitution may declare equality, but the courtroom has long recognized **hierarchy**.

Until now.

Because in the hands of an ordinary person, **AI has become the first tool to truly level the legal playing field**.

Not just in theory.

In function.

In form.

In **results**.

The Gap Between Principle and Practice

The Bill of Rights says you have a right to:

- Speak.
- Defend yourself.
- Confront your accuser.
- Not be deprived of life, liberty, or property without due process.

But what happens when:

- You can't afford a lawyer?
- You don't know which form to file?
- The court rules are in a dialect of Latin, legalese, and formatting hell?
- You make one mistake and lose your case forever?

Then those rights are not **rights**.

They're **privileges** reserved for the prepared—and **punishments** for everyone else.

AI: A Living Translator of Justice

The law was always meant to be public.

But it was never meant to be *understood.*

AI changes that.

It can:

- Translate a statute into plain English.
- Rephrase a legal demand in calm, persuasive tone.
- Draft a motion based on case facts and jurisdictional context.
- Explain deadlines, defenses, and discovery with precision.

It does for the courtroom what literacy once did for religion:
It takes the sacred text out of the hands of the few and gives it back to the people.

Due Process, Delivered at Last

True due process is not just about notice.

It's about **understanding**.

The AI-enabled litigant now has:

- The tools to file without confusion.
- The knowledge to argue without ridicule.
- The structure to be taken seriously.

For the first time, due process isn't dependent on whether you could afford a $400/hour gatekeeper.

It's about whether you can think, type, and persist—with a guide that never sleeps.

That's not science fiction.

That's already happening.

Equal Protection in Practice, Not Just Preamble

When AI helps a migrant understand eviction rights in their native language…

When AI helps a domestic violence survivor write a motion to extend protection…

When AI helps a wrongfully expelled club member document a pattern of retaliation…

That is equal protection.

Not in theory.

In court.

In cases.

In real lives.

AI Doesn't Just Fill Gaps—It Exposes Them

AI not only empowers the unheard. It reveals the **flaws of the system** itself:

- That court rules are arbitrarily inconsistent.
- That hearings are often about power, not merit.
- That pro se sanctions are more common than attorney ones—not because of conduct, but because of status.

- That corporations abuse legal shields, and no one notices until AI shines a spotlight.

In doing so, AI becomes **not just a helper—but a witness**.

A system that records, remembers, and reflects the contradictions in a process that was supposed to be blind—but never really was.

The Haberkorn Legacy: Constitutional Persistence

The Haberkorns were expelled without due process.

They were defamed without recourse.

They were sanctioned without recognition.

And yet, they filed.

With AI, they reconstructed timelines, challenged privilege, and documented injustice with the precision of a paralegal army.

They didn't win on paper.

But they **restored the record**.

They turned silence into a searchable archive of misconduct.

They proved that justice doesn't begin in a courtroom.

It begins with a prompt.

And ends with **a system forced to look itself in the mirror**.

Final Forecasts

- **By 2026**, states will pilot AI-informed civil access platforms.
- **By 2028**, AI-guided "public legal defenders" will be embedded in municipal legal aid.
- **By 2030**, equal protection case law will cite AI-empowered filings as examples of restored access.
- **By 2032**, courts will use AI to automatically notify litigants of procedural rights and formatting standards.
- **By 2035**, it will be malpractice *not* to consider AI assistance in ensuring fairness in pro se proceedings.

The promise of the Constitution was always beautiful.

But beauty without access is **performance**.

Now, AI makes that promise **real**.

Not just for lawyers.

Not just for corporations.

For **everyone** who was ever told, "You're not allowed to speak here."

Now they can speak.

Now they can file.

Now they can be heard.

Before we close this journey, pause with us in the **Timeline of Change**—a snapshot of the revolution already underway.

In this special section, we zoom out from chapters and arguments to trace the unfolding transformation in real time.
From the first public AI legal tools to the flood of pro se litigants entering courtrooms with code in their corner, this is the story of how justice is shifting—**month by month, motion by motion**.

History doesn't change all at once. It leaves breadcrumbs.

This interlude gathers them—so you can see not only where we've been, but where we're heading next.
The future has a timestamp. This is your guide.

"Equality before the law isn't a theory anymore. It's an interface."

— Prayer for Relief: ChatGPT

Timeline of Change

When the Future Became Inevitable

Technology rarely changes the law overnight. But once it begins to move, the shift is irreversible. First come the fringe cases, then the whispers in courtrooms, and finally—the rewriting of rules that once felt carved in stone.

This timeline is not just a forecast. It's a **warning**, a **promise**, and a **call to attention**. It maps the decade ahead, not as speculation, but as a **logical consequence**.

If you are a judge, a lawyer, a litigant, or simply someone who believes justice should be more than a slogan—**read this not as fiction**, but as the future arriving **faster than the system can prepare**.

◆ 2025: The Tipping Point Begins

- Bar associations begin debating the ethical use of generative AI in pleadings.
- First appellate court mentions a pro se litigant's AI-assisted filing as "notably structured."
- AI models offer real-time formatting assistance based on local court rules.

◆ 2026: Pro Se AI Litigants Gain Recognition

- State court systems pilot "AI Access Clinics" for self-represented individuals.

- Legal tech nonprofits launch guided prompt libraries for eviction, discrimination, and small claims.
- "Procedural inequality" becomes a policy issue in judicial conferences.

◆ **2027: Pro Se Majority Emerges**

- Over 50% of civil cases in urban jurisdictions are filed by pro se litigants using AI tools.
- Law review articles begin identifying "Prompt Law" as a formal discipline.
- Judges quietly begin clerking for AI summaries before hearing oral arguments.

◆ **2028: Legal Education Transforms**

- First ABA-accredited law school launches AI-integrated JD program.
- Law students attend "Prompt Clinics" instead of moot court.
- Legal internships include shadowing AI document review systems, not just partners.

◆ **2029: Corporate Privilege Faces Scrutiny**

- State legislatures propose bills limiting intra-corporate privilege when public harm is alleged.
- Discovery AI tools begin surfacing patterns of board misconduct in HOA and nonprofit disputes.
- Shareholder lawsuits reference AI-extracted patterns from prior dismissals.

2030: AI Becomes Judicial Co-Counsel

- Municipal courts deploy "Litigant Logic Assistants" (LLAs) to help parties prepare and file pre-trial documents.
- Clerks use AI dashboards to track incoming filings and triage motion complexity.
- Pro se litigants win landmark decisions, prompting judicial councils to revise access-to-justice metrics.

2031: Trust in the System Begins to Shift

- Public defenders incorporate ChatGPT-like tools in all non-criminal defense matters.
- National databases are built for AI-assisted filing templates across states.
- Court TV-style livestreams now include side-by-side commentary from AI that breaks down the legal action for public consumption.

2032: Constitutional Law Embraces AI

- A U.S. Supreme Court opinion references an AI-assisted pro se filing as part of its legal reasoning.
- Civil rights organizations deploy AI to help protestors file coordinated legal responses in real-time.
- Judges who repeatedly sanction pro se litigants without addressing their filings begin to appear on judicial watchlists—maintained by the public, not the system.

◆ 2033: The "Prompt Bar" Movement Begins

- Movements arise advocating certification of non-lawyers who demonstrate mastery of legal AI prompt systems.
- Alternative dispute resolution (ADR) platforms shift entirely to AI-guided workflows.
- Justice becomes faster, more accurate—and increasingly expected to be **open-source**.

◆ 2034: Law Without Lawyers?

- Over 70% of traffic, small claims, HOA, and disability claims are resolved without legal counsel.
- AI-supported self-representation becomes the norm in consumer fraud, discrimination, and defamation cases.
- Legal aid organizations train prompt specialists instead of paralegals.

◆ 2035: The Law Rewritten

- State and federal court rules formally recognize AI-supported pro se representation as a protected access right.
- A new legal branch is born: *Constitutional AI Rights*—addressing questions of equity, privacy, and access.
- And the Constitution, for the first time in history, **is read, understood, and acted on by every citizen who wants to file—not just the few who were licensed to interpret it.**

As we reach the end, **The Future Isn't Waiting** offers a closing truth for every reader—litigant, lawyer, club member, citizen.

This isn't just a book about what happened.
It's a signal flare for what's happening now—and what's coming fast.

Justice is no longer something you wait for.
It's something you can build, prompt by prompt, filing by filing, choice by choice.

In this final note, we invite you to step off the sidelines, pick up the tools now within reach, and become the advocate you once thought you had to hire.

Because the future of fairness is already arriving.
And this time, **you're in it.**

"You're not reading history. You're watching it unfold."

— Prayer for Relief: ChatGPT

The Future Isn't Waiting

If you're reading this in the present moment, you're already living in **the beginning** of what this timeline captures. This is not speculative fiction.

It is an outline of what happens when tools, truths, and courage collide.

It is what happens when pro se litigants refuse silence.

It is what happens when a book like *Prayer for Relief: ChatGPT* becomes not a guide—but **a prophecy made visible**.

Justice isn't just coming.

Justice is learning to write code.

And it's learning how to file.

In the **Prayer Answered?**, we return to the question that gave this book its name.

Has justice been done?
Can truth survive power?
Was the plea for fairness—so long ignored—finally heard?

This chapter doesn't offer easy answers. Instead, it offers something more enduring: a reckoning with what has changed, what still must change, and what it means to take your stand even when the odds say sit down.

Here, the legal fight becomes something bigger than filings and forums—it becomes a moral landmark, a signal to others, and perhaps, **a spark for the kind of justice that doesn't need permission to begin.**

"If you wait for the system to fix itself, you'll be waiting forever."

— Prayer for Relief: ChatGPT

Prayer Answered

From Silence to Filing, From Loss to Legacy

This book began with a fall.

A woman slipped on a neglected court.
A system ignored her.
Her husband spoke up.
And both were silenced.

The institutions closed ranks.
The courts turned pages but not ears.
And the truth—clear as daylight—was buried in technicalities and privilege.

But what Wilhelm and Susanne Haberkorn did next should be remembered—not for its pain, but for its **persistence**.

They did not vanish.

They documented.

They filed.

They **built a record the system could not erase**.

And they did it with a tool no one saw coming:

ChatGPT.

What This Book Is

Prayer for Relief: ChatGPT is more than a legal memoir. It is more than a toolkit. It is **a mirror held up to the American justice system**.

It shows us what happens when:

- Courts care more about procedure than people.
- Clubs care more about power than community.
- And lawyers care more about winning than what's right.

But it also shows us what can happen when a single voice finds its way back into the system—not through privilege, but through **persistence and precision**.

This book is the result of that effort.

You are holding the filings the courts ignored.

You are reading the evidence The Club never answered.

You are hearing the voice they tried to erase.

And now that voice is **speaking louder than ever**.

What You Can Do

If you've ever been:

- Expelled without cause.
- Sanctioned without defense.
- Silenced for telling the truth.

- Or treated as a "dependent" in a system you helped build…

Then this book is your **reminder**:
You are not powerless.

The law belongs to you, too.

And now, you have a way to speak it.

You can:

- Use the prompts.
- Follow the templates.
- Train with the tools.
- And build your own record—**not for sympathy, but for justice.**

This is not legal advice.

This is **legal strategy, translated**.

What the System Must Learn

To the judges who dismiss without reading: we are watching.

To The Clubs who expel without process: we are filing.

To the boards who call spouses "dependents": we are documenting.

To the corporations who hide behind privilege: we are prompting.

To the lawyers who scoff at pro se litigants: we are catching up—and **fast**.

Justice is not a favor.

It is a **right**.

And from this day forward, we will not ask.
We will **invoke**.
We will **plead**.
We will **file**.
And we will **pray for relief**—not from weakness, but from clarity and courage.

A Closing Prayer (for Real)

Let this be the last time a member is erased without cause.
Let this be the last time a court refuses to look.
Let this be the last time the truth is ignored because it came from the wrong name, the wrong format, the wrong person.

Let this be the first time **someone fights back with code and wins**.

And let that victory become contagious.

Because when the law is finally accessible to the people…

When the courtroom becomes a forum of equals…

When the robe listens as carefully to the pro se as to the silk-tied counsel…

That's not just justice.

That’s a **revolution**.

And it begins with one motion:

Prayer for Relief.

"When justice went silent, AI gave the people back their voice."

“They tried to erase a voice. Instead, they sparked a movement.”

— Prayer for Relief: ChatGPT

Appendix

Appendix A: FORUM Post
Appendix B: Expulsion Letter
Appendix C: Membership Agreement
Appendix D: All 16 Court Cases
Appendix E: All Cases – Paper Volume

Appendix A: FORUM Post

Anatomy of the 911 Landings Tennis Accident

On 9/11/2021, four members, Kathleen, Sue, Patty, and Susanne Haberkorn, engaged in their recurring Saturday tennis game. On one of the ball exchanges, Susanne Haberkorn tripped on the line tape, fell, and could not get up. The husband of Susanne Haberkorn was summoned off the golf course to the tennis courts to direct Chris Kader to get EMS for hospital evaluation. We made no provisions for determining the cause of the accident at that time. Securing medical treatment was the sole priority! A broken hip requiring hip replacement validated the taken course of action.

As a background, Susanne Haberkorn has played lots of tennis at The Club since 1998, conservatively greater than 5,000 hours without encountering a single trip and fall due to high line tapes. She was named super-woman by the TWATL in 2001 for being Senior Tennis and Senior Golf Club Champion that year.

The accident terminated her tennis career and converted an active player to subsiding the remaining tennis players every month.

How did Club and Members support our accident victim? Without going into the weeds of the problem, the highlights will do to enlighten the membership.
Kathleen offered two conflicting versions of the accident. One verification and one denial, having seen and not seen the accident!
The remaining players claimed not to have seen the accident is even more astonishing. All of that in a game that requires "Keeping your eyes on the ball at all times." For whatever reason, there seems to be "A Pragmatic Relationship with Truth!" Three Pinocchio's might be in order.

Then the response from our Executive Director, who reminded us not once but twice, "Reasonable risk is assumed in any athletic endeavor even on perfectly or reasonably maintained courts." De facto shifts the blame to the victim. Maybe there is a "Pragmatic Relationship with Responsibility?"

There was a shift in roles. The Club became the "Victim by being asked to take responsibility for high tapes" while the accident victim became the "Villain for asserting high tapes caused the accident!"

Not surprisingly, SELECTIVE INSURANCE COMPANY rejected any liability, and even more astonishing, all data used for the rejection are not accessible; they are secret. Access is only possible through **court order**!

Be it as it may, the best we can say about The Club's performance in that matter is a well-earned feckless.

What would a competent manager and organization do in such a case?

Any accident of such severity becomes the number one priority for the organization. Finding the root causes will prevent future accidents, as any organization needs to know that all accidents are preventable!

Communicate with the victim and the entire organization on an ongoing basis to show that the organization truly cares.

Work with the victim to map out mutually acceptable solutions.

Work with external resources to harvest more or missing expertise, but do not abdicate management and control responsibilities. Our leaders get paid for dealing with a lack of expert knowledge and uncertainty.

None of that happened in the 911 trip, fall, and hip replacement case.

Recommendation for any future accident victim

Trust nobody.
Document, document, document.
Get a qualified lawyer.

Appendix B: Expulsion Letter

July 29, 2022

Mr. Wilhelm Haberkorn (#4455)
4 Painted Bunting Lane
Savannah, Georgia 31411

Dear Mr. Haberkorn,
The Board of Governors of The Club has received a complaint about your misuse of the online Member Forum on July 27, 2022, to inappropriately and publicly voice your opinion concerning an issue you have with the conduct of The Club and its members. In your post to the Member Forum, you publicly disparaged Club staff and several fellow members. You were notified of this infraction by Mr. Steven Freund on July 27, the post was removed from the Forum, and your privileges to The Club electronic media were suspended. On that same day, the infraction was referred to the Member Standards Committee. The Board of Governors has received the Committee's recommendation and has determined that your actions violate The Club Bylaws and Rules and Regulations as follows:

Club Bylaws Article XIII-Discipline:
A. 3. *"Unsatisfactory behavior, conduct, or appearance."*
A. 10. *"Treatment of the personnel or employees of The Club in an unreasonable or abusive manner."*

Club Rules and Regulations:
Section I, Paragraph 4, A. 3. *"Exhibits unsatisfactory behavior, conduct, or appearance."*
Section I, Paragraph 4, A. 7. *"Treats a member, personnel or employees of The Club in a disrespectful, disparaging, or abusive manner."*
On July 28, the Board of Governors met to review the findings and recommendations of the
Member Standards Committee. It is the Board's decision that you be expelled from The Club upon receipt of this letter. In part, the decision was based on your improper use of the

member roster that occurred in January 2022. As a result of that incident, you received a letter of reprimand which specifically stated, "*Any further instances of unacceptable behavior, including further harassment of Governors or Club staff on your part, could result in suspension or expulsion under the Bylaws.*"

Other factors considered were: the amount of Club resources that have been used to respond to your continuing threats to bring legal action against your Landings Club, the severity of your inappropriate behavior, the amount of hostility you have shown to members and Club staff, your complete disregard for Club rules, and your lack of remorse for any of your actions, as communicated by you to the staff and other members.

Landings Club Bylaws, Article XIII, Discipline, Paragraph

E. Expulsion, reads as follows:

"*A Member may be expelled or suspended by The Club if the Board determines that the Member's conduct was improper or likely to endanger the welfare, safety, harmony or good reputation of The Club or its Members. Any Member who has been expelled shall not again be eligible for Membership nor admitted to The Club's property under any circumstances. A Member who has been expelled from The Club shall forfeit his or her Membership in The Club and in the sole discretion of the Board of Governors, may not be entitled to the return of any Membership costs or other dues and fees previously paid to The Club.*"

You are also not entitled to be a guest at The Club or be on its property at any time.

You are entitled to appeal this decision to the Board of Governors. If you desire to be heard by the Board, you must provide a written request for a hearing to the Board within fifteen (15) days of receipt of notice of this action. Upon the Board's receipt of the written request for a hearing, the Board shall set a time and date not less than ten (10) days thereafter for such a hearing. Any correspondence should be sent to the attention of Michael Barber at The Club office at 71 Green Island Road, Savannah, GA 31411.

The Board of Governors has thoroughly reviewed all accounts of this incident and has seriously and solemnly come to this conclusion.

Our documentation system requires a signed receipt of this letter of notification. To avoid any further emotional issues for your wife, you are required to receive and sign for a paper copy of this letter at the front desk of The Club Operations Office on Green Island Road within three (3)
business days of the date of this electronic notice. If you have not signed for the letter by close of business on the third day, the paper copy will be sent directly to your residence.

Sincerely,

Michael Barber, President, The Club Board of Governors

cc: Robert Hainly, Chair, Member Standards Committee
Steven Freund, Executive Director
Gary Lorfano, Membership Director
Mary Morgan, Membership Relations Manager

Appendix C: Membership Agreement

MEMBERSHIP PURCHASE AGREEMENT

The undersigned applies for an Equity Membership in The Landings Club, Inc. (the "Club") and agrees to pay to **The Landings Club, Inc.** the membership price for the membership category selected below.

Check One	Category	Membership Price
✓	Golf	$35,000
___	Tennis	$12,000
___	Social	$ 7,000

Please submit a check for the full amount of the membership price, made payable to The Landings Club, Inc., along with this Membership Purchase Agreement and the Application for Membership.

The undersigned understands that this Membership Purchase Agreement is irrevocable after mailing or delivery to the Club, unless the undersigned is not approved for membership.

No membership certificate shall be issued until the undersigned has been approved for membership.

The undersigned hereby acknowledges receipt of a copy of the Plan for The Offering Of Memberships in The Landings Club, Inc., dated May 19, 1989, and the Modification of Membership Plan Documents, dated June 23, 1989, (collectively, the "Membership Plan"), and agrees to be bound by all their respective terms and conditions.

If the undersigned is approved for membership, the undersigned agrees to be bound by the Membership Plan and irrevocably agrees to fully substitute the membership privileges acquired pursuant to this Membership Purchase Agreement for any present or prior right to or use of the Club Facilities.

If the Applicants are married the signatures of both spouses are required.

Please indicate desired dues category and billing status here.

✓ Active ___ Non-Resident Limited To be Billed: ___ Annually ___ Quarterly ✓ Monthly

Wilhelm A. Haberkorn — Please Print Name

Susanne N. Haberkorn — Please Print Name

[signature] — Applicant's Signature

[signature] — Applicant's Signature

_______ — Dated

1-10-98 — Dated

Susanne N. Haberkorn W. A. Haberkorn

Indicate name(s) listed on property deed. This name(s) will be listed on the Membership Certificate.

clear 1/28/98

Reviewed by: [signature] 1/26/98
Director of Membership — Date

Approved by: Patricia S. Pullen 1-26-98
Membership Committee Chairperson — Date

Appendix D: All 16 Court Cases

Case Filed Date	Case Description	Case Number
10/12/2024	Wilhelm A. Haberkorn, Susanne N. Haberkorn vs Bob Hainly	STCV24-02347
10/12/2024	Wilhelm A. Haberkorn, Susanne N. Haberkorn vs Kathleen Ihnat, Sue Anderson	STCV24-02346
8/1/2024	Wilhelm Haberkorn and Susanne Haberkorn vs The Landings Club Inc.	SPCV24-00915-co
7/10/2023	Wilhelm A. Haberkorn, Susanne Haberkorn vs The Landings Club Inc. Member Standards Committee	STCV23-01395
7/3/2023	Wilhelm A. Haberkorn, Susanne Haberkorn vs The Landings Club Inc.	STCV23-01367
6/16/2023	Wilhelm A. Haberkorn, Susanne Haberkorn vs Steven Freund	STCV23-01240
5/13/2023	Wilhelm A. Haberkorn, Susanne Haberkorn vs Mary Beth McGirr	STCV23-01007
5/13/2023	Wilhelm A. Haberkorn, Susanne Haberkorn vs Bob Lindenschmidt	STCV23-01006
5/13/2023	Wilhelm A. Haberkorn, Susanne Haberkorn vs Dick Oswald	STCV23-01008

Case Filed Date	Case Description	Case Number
5/13/2023	Wilhelm A. Haberkorn, Susanne Haberkorn vs Jack Welch	STCV23-01009
5/12/2023	Wilhelm A. Haberkorn, Susanne Haberkorn vs Bob Hainly	STCV23-01005
5/12/2023	Wilhelm A. Haberkorn, Susanne Haberkorn vs Mike Stephens	STCV23-01002
5/12/2023	Wilhelm A. Haberkorn, Susanne Haberkorn vs Nancy Early	STCV23-01001
5/11/2023	Wilhelm A. Haberkorn, Susanne Haberkorn vs Ken Ura	STCV23-00993
5/3/2023	Wilhelm A. Haberkorn, Susanne Haberkorn vs Michael Barber	STCV23-00904
4/20/2023	Susanne N. Haberkorn, Wilhelm A. Haberkorn vs Select Insurance Company	STCV23-00838

Appendix E: All Cases - Paper Volume

Case Filed Date	Case Number	Filings	Pages
10/12/2024	STCV24-02347	7	47
1 0/12/2024	STCV24-02346	13	67
8/1/2024	SPCV24-00915-co	218	2,178
7/10/2023	STCV23-01395	60	675
7/3/2023	STCV23-01367	0	0
6/16/2023	STCV23-01240	108	1,567
5/13/2023	STCV23-01007	107	1,463
5/13/2023	STCV23-01006	106	1,463
5/13/2023	STCV23-01008	107	1,463
5/13/2023	STCV23-01009	107	1,463
5/12/2023	STCV23-01005	107	1,463
5/12/2023	STCV23-01002	108	1,463
5/12/2023	STCV23-01001	105	1,463

Case Filed Date	Case Number	Filings	Pages
5/11/2023	STCV23-00993	6	170
5/3/2023	STCV23-00904	105	1,463
4/20/2023	STCV23-00838	32	137
Total		**1,296**	**16,545**

www.ingramcontent.com/pod-product-compliance
Lightning Source LLC
LaVergne TN
LVHW090310210926
848480LV00001B/200

* 9 7 9 8 2 3 0 0 9 3 6 3 3 *